RAJASTHAN

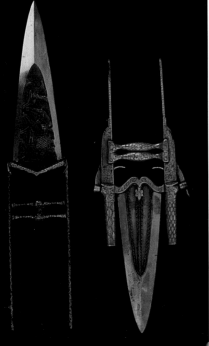

All rights reserved. No part of this publication may be transmitted or reproduced in any form or by any means without prior permission from the publisher.

Text: Sunil Mehra © Lustre Press
Introduction: Kishore Singh © Lustre Press
Photographs: Pramod Kapoor, Karoki Lewis © Lustre Press

ISBN: 81-7436-059-x

Published by
Roli Books Pvt. Ltd.
Lustre Press Pvt. Ltd.
M-75, Greater Kailash II Market
New Delhi - 110 048, India
Tel: (011) 6442271, 6462782
Fax: (011) 6467185

Reprinted 1998, 2001

Text Editor: Kishore Singh
Picture Editor: Pramod Kapoor

Printed and bound at
Star Standard Industries Pte. Ltd. Singapore

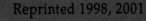

Front jacket: *The picture depicts Maharaja Gaj Singh II of Jodhpur, on his birthday, as he holds court, going through the annual custom of making gifts and donations.* **Half-title page:** *The head of the fief of Madhogarh; over two hundred such aristocrats once paid allegiance to the royal house of Jaipur.* **Title page:** *A collage of Rajputana impressions.* **Contents page:** *Women dress festively to attend the annual fair at Pushkar.*

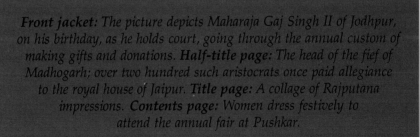

Rajasthan

An Enduring Romance

Text
Sunil Mehra

Photographs
Pramod Kapoor
Karoki Lewis

Lustre Press
Roli Books

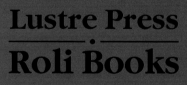

To my mother and sister who taught me about loving and giving;
To Habbu, from whom I learnt much and who made this possible;
To Chiku, Umar and Usman who gave moral support as only friends can;
Last, but not the least, for Kishore, who kept faith.

CONTENTS

A JOURNEY INTO RAJASTHAN

The splendour of the Rajput courts at an early period of the history of that country, making every allowance for the exaggeration of the bards, must have been great. It has abounded in the more striking events that constitute the materials for history; there is not a petty State in Rajasthan that has not had its Thermopylae, and scarcely a city that has not produced its Leonidas.
— Col. James Tod

Colourfully dressed Bishnoi women in their rural habitat. The necklaces, called 'timaniya', and the crescent moon-shaped, bejewelled nose rings are customarily worn by all married Bishnoi women.

Top: Udaipur by night. To the left, set in the Lake Pichola, is the 18th-century Lake Palace; to the right is the 16th-century City Palace which also houses the Shiv Niwas Palace hotel. Above: A Kalbeliya dancer swirls gracefully in the ornate Durbar hall at Samode Palace hotel near Jaipur.

sents. They travelled to London, where they had accounts at all the major stores, suites at the best hotels, and were entertained by the King and Queen. In a few generations they had moved from being actual rulers to merely assuming the trappings of kingship; true power rested in British hands, not theirs.

That was princely Rajasthan—but there is also the more visible, equally intriguing, easily accessible everyday Rajasthan. There is pride here too, the flash of colour and the cloak of ritual. The Rajasthani aesthetic sensibility transforms humble homes into living art galleries; music, festivity accompanies all celebrations and events, from social and religious fairs to commerce, from marriage to the birth of a child; from the onset of the rains to the offerings of sacrifices before fierce goddesses. While the warrior-Rajput revels in the chase of the hunt, the conservationist-Bishnoi spends his life in the protection of everything from trees to blackbuck, while inviting visitors to his home with cupped palms full of opium.

What, then, are a visitor's impressions of this state, which offers a valid contradiction to almost every statement it makes? First, there are its forts and palaces, its temples and mansions, in an amazing number and variety. Within beautiful palaces where narrow staircases impeded the entry of ravaging armies are apartments adorned with some of the country's best-known schools of painting; gilded halls where the rulers held court; pleasure pavilions with *sileh-khanas* (armouries) that are now museums. The later palaces are often hotels, some even with maharajas in residence. There are festivals and crafts—and the people themselves, colourful and vibrant. And there is the landscape, composed almost entirely of sand dunes that shift restlessly in the breeze. Ris-

ing from this sea of sand is the Aravalli range of hills where the princes once went hunting, and where tigers and game are still to be found, though they are now protected by law. Surprisingly, Rajasthan also has lakes and pools, streams and rivers; hills and forests, and fields where water is abundant. Its ancient forts have been abandoned to the desert, or surrounded by cities, but far out in the wilderness where the wind moves continually—sometimes chill, sometimes sere— the history of a valiant land lies buried in the sands, even as the present recreates the past in a pageant of splendour and celebration.

And what celebration! There are fairs that have endured since as long as memory serves and before; since time immemorial, when the gods walked upon the earth...year after year, the cycle of commerce, religion and social interaction continues. No one, for instance, knows the history of Pushkar's annual cattle fair, but the locals tell of the life and times of Brahma, the Creator, and how he came to this solitary temple dedicated to him in the town since sanctified by his presence. Or the processions: once led by kings, they are every bit as resplendent now as they step out of their city forts and palaces on occasions such as Gangaur and Teej. These

events occur all year round, and the calendar moves from folk revelry to formal festivity, from public participation to private ceremony. In the rhythm of this ancient land the celebration of life and the past endures, and the present belongs to the future.

Nobility and the hoi polloi gather in the erstwhile ballroom of the pink Umaid Bhawan palace to greet Maharaja Gaj Singh of Jodhpur, seated on a low divan *(center right), and offer the customary* nazar *or tribute on his birthday.*

CITY OF AUTUMNAL SUNSET

Jaipur, Ajmer, Kishangarh

There is an interesting incident concerning Duleh Rai, who was routed at Manch by the Meenas. Lying wounded, the chieftain had a vision of Goddess Jammuva Mata urging him once more to battle for, she predicted, victory would be his, after which he should lay the foundation of his capital there. As she had prophesied, so it was, and at the spot where he had lain fatigued by battle still stands a temple dedicated to Jammuva Mata, the family deity of the Jaipur Kachwahas.
— Rajmata Gayatri Devi

Maharaja Bhawani Singh of Jaipur offering prayers outside the Hall of Public Audience in the City Palace on his birthday. Family retainers stand behind him holding the royal standards and the yak-tail 'chamar', or fan.

The pink city of Jaipur that rises like a mirage from the tawny Aravalli landscape is the present-day capital of Rajasthan, but for almost two hundred and fifty years this was the capital of the Kachwaha Rajputs, descendants of Rama (hero of the epic Ramayana). Their story began in 961 AD in distant Narwar, now in Madhya Pradesh; they had ruled here for eight hundred years, till the infant ruler Dhola Rae's throne was usurped by his uncle. The widowed queen fled to nearby Khagaon, where the tribal Mina raja adopted her as his sister and Dhola Rae as his nephew.

Dhola Rae did to the Mina raja what his uncle had done to him — he usurped his throne and murdered him in the bargain. A matrimonial alliance with a Dausa princess, whose father gifted him that kingdom as well, further enhanced his financial resources. The Minas got their revenge soon enough, when they waylaid and killed Dhola Rae at Jamva Ramgarh, close to Amber. His second wife escaped to give birth to a child, and the wheel came full circle when her grandson wrested Amber from the Sushwat Minas around 1150; here he laid the foundations of the great Kachwaha empire which reigned for the next six centuries.

A palace retainer framed against the peacock motif gateway with fine repousse brass door at City Palace, Jaipur.

By the end of the 12th century, the Kachwahas were a power to reckon with. They understood realpolitik, and the moment the political balance shifted in favour of the Mughals, they forged an alliance that catapulted them from local chieftains to a position of sub-continental pre-eminence. The 16th century Amber chief Baharmal was the first Rajput to pay homage to Humayun. He set the example of the typical Rajput-Mughal exchange — Humayun gave Baharmal command of a 5,000 strong army, while the latter gave his daughter in marriage to Humayun's son, Akbar, and placed his adopted grandson Man Singh in Mughal service.

The Mughal-Kachwaha relationship was further cemented by Bhagwan Das, Baharmal's successor, who won Akbar's abiding gratitude by saving his life in the battle of Sarwal. A second matrimonial alliance ensued in 1585-86 when Bhagwan Das married his daughter to Salim, the eldest son of Akbar. Akbar's reciprocal gift was generous — a command of 5,000 horse and the governorship of Punjab.

Amber's power peaked under Man Singh I and Jai Singh I, who rendered singular service to the Mughal emperor. Man Singh was one of Akbar's most powerful generals and reigned at various stages as governor of Bengal, Bihar, Kabul and the Deccan. Ties of blood naturally led him to support his nephew Khusrau in the battle of succession that started even as Akbar lay on his death bed. The emperor's anointed successor Jehangir triumphed, but not before he had bought peace from this erstwhile vassal turned arbiter of the empire's destiny with a bribe equivalent to almost one million pounds sterling. Man Singh's avarice earned Jaipur the title of *Chor Durbar* (court of thieves).

Following Man Singh's death in distant Deccan, Jaipur went into a temporary political eclipse until the arrival of the brilliant warrior and strategist Mirza Raja Jai Singh in 1625-67. He came to the throne at eleven; by thirteen he was commanding an army of three thousand in the Deccan. Consideration of moral principles were laid aside when he shrewdly backed Aurangzeb and betrayed the unfortunate Dara Shikoh in the battle for the Mughal throne that broke out during Shah Jahan's lifetime. Aurangzeb rewarded him with a command of seven thousand horse — an honour hitherto reserved for members of the royal family alone. He captured Shivaji for Aurangzeb, but later enraged the emperor by contriving the Maratha leader's escape when he realised the crafty Aurangzeb was planning to renege on an earlier promise that Shivaji would not be done away with. Aurangzeb connived to have Mirza Raja Jai Singh murdered by his own younger son, promising him Amber — a promise he characteristically reneged on once his purpose was successfully accomplished.

It was against the backdrop of this hostile political situation that Sawai Jai Singh came to the throne in 1699. The eleven-year-old duly went to pay homage to the Mughal emperor Aurangzeb in Delhi. The ageing Mughal grasped the young man's hands and asked him how he expected to be as powerful as his predecessor if his hands were tied thus. Young Jai Singh was, but tactless he was not, and pat came his reply—when a bridegroom takes the bride's hand, he is bound to protect her for life; thus, after such a royal gesture, would not the Mughal protect him forever? This endearing riposte ensured the cessation of Mughal hostility towards Amber.

Jai Singh was a multi-faceted man: a political Machiavelli; a warrior par excellence; a scientist, administrator, astronomer and town planner. By age thirteen he had devised an irrigation system to water the hanging gardens at Amber; at fourteen he defeated the Marathas for the Mughals at the battle of Khalna, earning himself the title of Sawai. A political miscalculation after Aurangzeb's death in 1707 almost cost him the throne of Amber. He backed Azam Shah, who lost the battle for succession. The suspicious victor Bahadur Shah promptly dispatched his envoy to take over Amber, which he did; but Jai Singh, sword in hand, evicted the usurper and reclaimed his territory. He re-united the powerful Rajput states against the Mughal and threw them out of Jodhpur. A troublesome younger brother and Mughal ally was ruthlessly murdered, and Sawai Jai Singh was once again firmly in command.

With peace and security came the motivation to indulge himself and his intellectual passions. The result was Jaipur — The first planned city in India, its foundation stone was laid in November 1727. Jaisingh was aided by a young Bengali engineer and scholar named Vidyadhar Bhattacharya, who devised a spacious and elegant city built on a simple grid system. Seven blocks of buildings were divided by wide, tree-lined avenues, each building embellished by an ordered variety of architectural decorations. At its heart lay the city palace covering the space of two blocks. The entire city was surrounded by seven formidable gates which were closed at night to ensure security against maruders. Late into this century, these gates were locked at 11pm leaving passengers arriving by night trains stranded outside the city till daybreak. The king offered concessions to traders and artisans, invited businessmen to settle in Jaipur and made it obligatory for all local chieftains to build houses with state patronage and, of course, prior approval of building plans by Vidyadhar. He specified localities for different artisans within his walled capital and recognised trade guilds.

The socio-political situation during the ensuing years helped the growth of the city. The Sikhs had paralysed the trade routes passing through the Punjab, and the frequent invasions of Ahmed Shah Abdali at Delhi, Agra and Mathura had struck terror into the hearts of Jain merchants, who flocked to this new commercial haven, where they received a warm welcome. A royal department monitored the purity and standard of jewels and jewellery manufactured in Jaipur through a system of fines and incentives. As early as 1835 Jaipur was exporting precious stones to Europe. Today, almost forty thousand gem-cutters work in areas known as Gopalji ka Rasta and Haldiyon ka Rasta, cutting and polishing stones that are crafted into exquisite jewellery and sold in Johari Bazaar. Many of them are descendants of the five enamellers' families invited by Man Singh to come and settle in Amber. From here they moved to Jaipur, today considered the gem and jewellery capital of the world.

The epicentre of the new city was obviously the royal complex with its beautiful

One of the two silver water-flasks taken by the 19th century Jaipur ruler, Madho Singh, when he went to England to attend Edward VII's coronation.

The 18th century Hawa Mahal at Jaipur was built by Maharaja Pratap Singh of Jaipur. The five-storeyed, pink-sandstone structure with 553 niches and windows covered with lace screens, served as a grandstand for the royal ladies. In a fitting tribute to architect Lal Usta's genius, his descendants remain exempt from paying taxes to the present day.

including Lutyens, who built New Delhi. This museum today houses manuscripts, medieval weapons, Persian carpets, and curiosities such as an Egyptian mummy.

The all-pervasive pink of Jaipur, visible on all houses facing main streets, was the idea of 19th century ruler Maharaja Ram Singh. Some buildings were pink, and Ram Singh tried white, green and yellow before finally deciding on the pink colour wash for the whole city, apparently to welcome the Prince of Wales during his visit to the city.

Moti Doongri Palace, situated atop a small hillock next to the university is a tiny fort that gives the appearance of a Scottish castle and whose luxurious interiors were furnished with Louis XIV furniture. The personal Kachwaha treasure was stored here at least till 1975, when taxmen swooped down to confiscate gold and jewellery worth almost six billion dollars, but which to their disappointment turned out to be documented and legitimate.

Barely half a kilometre from Moti Doongri is Rambagh Palace, a luxury hotel that until a few decades ago was home to the fairytale couple that was the toast of British society — the polo-playing Maharaja Man Singh II and Maharani Gayatri Devi, popularly known as Jai and Ayesha. This was Ram Singh's hunting lodge which a successor, Madho Singh II, transformed, with the help of Swinton Jacob, into a palace with formal English gardens, tennis and squash courts, and an indoor swimming pool, complete with art-deco embellishments. Much of its later glamour came when Jai and Ayesha moved in: marble and Lalique fountains, London-designed drawing rooms, boldly geometric furnishings, a handsome bar with an indoor fountain and sepia-tinted photographs and trophies won during polo matches still create an atmosphere of opulence.

En route to Amber lies Man Sagar, a large artificial lake with the Jal Mahal, a pleasure palace, set in its middle, once the scene for aristocratic duck shoots. Further up the road, atop a jagged hill, is Nahargarh fort. This was where the royal treasure was housed before Man Singh II moved it to Moti Doongri, and

it was to this mountain-top resort that Jai Singh's maharanis retreated to relax and savour the spectacular sunset views of the city that stretches below. Built in the 18th century to defend the new city, it was also used as a pleasure resort by the dissolute Jagat Singh who almost provoked a rebellion when he ensconced his concubine, Raskafur, here, struck gold coins in her name, and declared her queen of half of Amber. The highlight of the fort is a complex network of scientifically designed canals that collected and carried rainwater to large reservoirs at Nahargarh and the adjacent fort of Jaigarh.

Cheek by jowl with Amber lies the fort of Jaigarh built by Jai Singh in 1726. Here are the remains of an ancient foundry where cannons were cast — among them the massive Jaiwan cannon that could allegedly fire a cannonball to a distance of almost 40 km. Originally this housed the Kachwaha treasure zealously guarded by Mina tribesmen, and popular legend would have it that each new ruler was led blindfolded to the treasury, from where he could pick just one

souvenir. The last ruler Man Singh II apparently picked a jewelled bird with two giant rubies for eyes. The bird exists, but the rubies are missing; so is the treasure, though in 1976 taxmen spent six months digging for it. Locals insist Sawai Jai Singh II used it up to build his opulent city; credulous believers of the legend insist it is still there.

There is a wild, romantic beauty about Amber. Strategically, the fort is well placed, commanding an eagle's eye-view of the gorge formed by the range called the 'Kalikoh'. Within lies Man Singh's 16th century Kali temple dedicated to Shila Mata, whose image he brought back from Jessore in Bengal and enshrined amid green marble pillars carved in the shape of plantain trees; the solid silver entrance doors were built by the 19th century ruler Man Singh II in gratitude for having survived a plane crash.

The most arresting vision in Amber is that of the splendid hall of public audience, set on a dazzling white terrace with a sweeping view of the gorge below. Delicately carved columns with elephant capitals support a

The Sheesh Mahal at Amber whose interior is encrusted with tiny mirrors. The hall when closed and lit by candles resembles a huge, twinkling diamond.

Below: Rajmata Gayatri Devi of Jaipur.
Bottom: The Jaipur royals inherited their passion for polo from their Jodhpur cousins. Madho Singh II was an enthusiast and his successor Raja Mansingh II's Jaipur polo team swept all the matches in Britain in the 1930s.

Facing page: Maharaja Bhawani Singh of Jaipur being greeted by noble-women at Chandra Mahal in the City Palace during his birthday celebrations.

vaulted canopy. Shah Jahan was almost tetchy in a firman he sent to Jaipur; he demanded that Mirza Raja Jai Singh send his sculptors to the capital so that they could work on the Taj Mahal instead of 'detaining them in Amber'. Indeed, the delicacy was so much to the Mughal taste that Jai Singh ordered his masons to cover it with stucco before the envious emperor's commissioners arrived to see it. Now, with the stucco starting to wear off, the decoration has begun to be revealed.

The majestic Ganesh Pole leads to the garden court Sukh Niwas, so called because of its cleverly designed system of (airconditioned) apartments. Jai Mandir contains the Sheesh Mahal and the Diwan-i-Khas. The former, inlaid with tiny, winking glass mosaics set at all angles, is a splendid sight when the doors are closed and candles lit to allow the ceiling its accurate imitation of the night sky with a thousand glittering stars. The latter is painted with delicate murals of flowers, leafy scrolls and designs of lamps and goblets in a mixture of green and turquoise. The doors are of sandal-wood inlaid with ivory. On the top storey is Jal Mahal; its latticed windows offer a marvellous view of the garden set in the middle of Maota Lake at the base of the fort where saffron once grew.

Vidyadhar, the co-architect of Jaipur, was awarded a ceremonial robe of honour and an elephant named Meera Gaj for his splendid achievements. Eight kilometres from the city lies Vidyadharji ka Bagh, a sprawling garden interspersed with pleasant pavilions. Close by is Sisodia Rani ka Bagh, a garden-palace built for his Udaipur queen by Jai Singh II in the 18th century. Fine terrace gardens with fountains and statues; glorious murals of hunting scenes, strolling lovers and vignettes from the lives of Radha and Krishna contribute to an ethereal vision of beauty.

Sleepy Ajmer, 80 km from Jaipur, now better known as a Muslim pilgrimage centre, was once the proud capital of the Chauhan Rajputs who ruled Delhi in the 7th century. The city derives its name from Ajaipal who built what was among the earliest of Rajput fortresses, Taragarh, atop the mountains called Ajaimeru. Ajmer's fortunes fluctuated with those of the Chauhans, after whose defeat by Mohammad Ghori in the 12th century its ownership see-sawed between Mewar and Marwar for almost four centuries until the Mughal Emperor Akbar annexed it in 1556 and made the city his strategic military base in Rajputana. Ajmer was important to Akbar — it housed the shrine of the fabled Khwaja Moinuddin Chishti, the Sufi mystic to whose final resting place he walked twice all the way from Agra to pray for the fulfilment of a cherished desire: the birth of a male heir. This was Salim who went on to rule as Emperor Jehangir, and who also lived in Ajmer from 1613 to 1616; his fabulous Daulat Bagh palace here now lies in ruins. The Mughals' imperial connection with Ajmer weakened with time as Ajmer went first into Maratha and later British hands in the 19th century. Its spiritual connection endured, however, for the emotional link with the Chishti shrine was strong and abiding.

Chishti came with Mohammad Ghori's army from Persia in the 12th century and stayed on to found his Sufi order. Emperors and commoners alike flocked to his shrine, considered a place of wish-fulfilment for the faithful who pray with a true heart. The humble grave of the Sufi who spurned ostentation is today surrounded by a silver railing and partly by a marble screen. Adjacent to the shrine is a mosque built in his honour by Akbar, while to its west lies a pearly white house of prayer raised by Shah Jahan, whose devout daughter constructed the delicately

beautiful prayer house for women devotees next to it.

There are two huge cauldrons, nine feet in diameter, in which sanctified food donated by the faithful is cooked during holy days. The original cauldrons were gifted by Akbar and Jehangir but were subsequently replaced in the 19th century. The sanctified food is sold to the followers of this protector of the poor and downtrodden, or Khwaja

The 17th-century Jaiwana cannon built at the foundry in Jaigarh fort. Purportedly the largest cannon in Asia, this was probably never tried for it would need an area the size of a football field to accommodate the recoil!

Garib Nawaz, as the saint is called.

A little away from the city is the Adhai Din ka Jhonpra (two and a half days' shed). In the process of converting the building — originally a college of Sanskrit learning — into a mosque in 1198, the Muslim king Mohammad Ghori left a fascinating documentation of both Hindu and Muslim architectural styles of that period. The surface decorations and ornate calligraphic inscriptions are superlative examples of Islamic architecture. The pillars he could not alter survive as superb examples of ornamentation in the Hindu tradition. The peculiar name of the monument dates from the 18th century when *fakirs* used to congregate here for the martyrdom ceremony that used to last two and a half days.

Modern Ajmer is no longer known for the musk roses that were first distilled into 'attar' (a perfume concentrate) here, but for its Mayo College, the school for Rajput royalty established by the British in 1874. Its first pupil was the maharaja of Alwar.

Nineteen kilometres from Ajmer on the Jaipur road lies a pretty town with cobbled streets, veritable carpets of red chillies drying on the road side and tiny ateliers where artists turn out pale imitations of Rajput miniature paintings. This tiny 17th century kingdom was founded by the youngest brother of the maharaja of Jodhpur, but remained politically insignificant. It was only in 1940, when the royal family first exhibited its fabulous collection of Rajasthani miniatures to awestruck art critics in India and abroad that the international art market sat up and took notice of Kishangarh. Almost unknown to the world, this tiny kingdom had nurtured one of the finest schools of miniature paintings in 18th century India.

In the 17th and 18th centuries, with dwindling imperial patronage in Delhi, artists from the famed Mughal ateliers had started looking for newer pastures. The exodus was considerably accelerated by the orthodox Islamic Emperor Aurangzeb, for whom any representation of a living form was blasphemy. Renowned painters such as Surat Ram and Nihal Chand came to settle in Kishangarh around this time. The initial creative impulse was carefully nurtured by the aesthetically inclined Raja Satwant Singh, whose lady love and mistress, the aquiline-nosed, lotus-eyed Bani Thani was allegedly the inspiration and model for innumerable miniatures of Radha painted by the artists at the royal atelier. Later, in 1757, Satwant Singh abdicated and retired to Vrindaban with his paramour. With this presumably the Kishangarh school of painting also went into decline.

Today artists in narrow bylanes evoke nostalgia for the days when Kishangarh paintings rivalled those of the Kangra school in excellence. The tiny palace in the middle of Kishangarh's lake is strongly reminiscent of that in Udaipur. A palace and fort overlook the lake, where weeds and lotuses bloom and ducks and egrets swim and squabble, evoking a feeling of nostalgia tinged with regret at the lost splendour of Kishangarh.

Kishangarh beckons like a voice from the past and has the haunting, evocative quality of a beautiful but shattered dream...

Rajasthani Turbans

Called a safa, paag or pagri, the turban is the most visible part of a man's dress, and in Rajasthan perhaps the most important. The average length of a turban is nine metres, though it can sometimes be twice as long. Saffron is the colour of chivalry, and therefore turbans of this colour are worn at weddings; in the past warriors would go to battle clad in saffron headgear. While white, dark blue, khaki, maroon and black turbans are worn during periods of mourning, the Bishnoi community wears white turbans at all times.

While the turban itself is worn as protection aginst the sun, it has also come to symbolise

honour — knocked over, it implies an insult; placed at another man's feet, it suggests complete surrender; an exchange of turbans signifies a bond of brotherhood . When a man carries a turban in his hands to present to a woman, it tells of her husband's death. Illustrated on this page are turbans from all over Rajasthan. Left column, top to bottom : Jalori, from Jhalore ; Bhatti from Jaisalmer ; the 'Shahi' Jodhpur paag ; the Jaisalmer merchants' pagri ; the paag from Banswara ; and a shepherd's turban. Right column, top to bottom: the distinctive Alwar turban ; the 'Darbari' paag from Dholpur ; the hunting 'Shikari' headgear of Udaipur ; the neat Sirohi turban ; the Jaipuri turban from Jaipur; the Jodhpuri safa that is now worn all over Rajasthan.

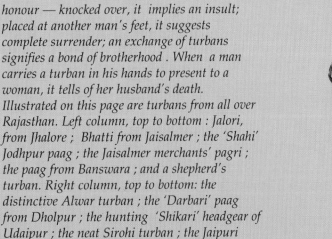

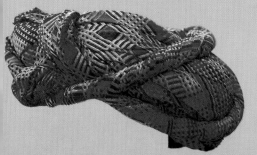

PUSHKAR

Come November, and Hindu devotees head towards the 8th century shrine of Pushkar, seven miles from Ajmer. A winding hill road leads to the ancient lake that is supposed to have appeared miraculously on the spot where Brahma the Creator dropped a lotus from his hand. An amusing anecdote is recounted about Pushkar Lake: when Brahma found that there was no edifice to his name on the earth he had created, he formed this lake with the appropriate adjunct that any devotee bathing in its waters would be guaranteed entry into heaven. Soon thereafter, and naturally, heaven became crowded, at which point fellow-gods implored Brahma to curtail his largesse, if not withdraw it. At this Brahma relented and restricted entry into heaven to those devotees who bathed in the lake during the four specified days of Kartik Purnima...hence the rush to bathe in the holy waters during the four days in November.

Preceding page:
Portrait of a woman at the fair.
Preceding page, inset:
The tortoise is worshipped as Brahma's mount.
Top: *An aerial view of Pushkar town.*

Over the years this great religious fair became an occasion for the simple-minded villagers who flocked here annually to not only procure salvation but also good prices for their bullocks, horses and camels, as well as suitable matches for eligible sons and daughters—thus admirably combining spiritual and temporal concerns. Pushkar offers an unforgettable spectacle of people in all their spontaneous joy and colour, and of devotees floating oil lamps on the waters of the lake on a dark night in a centuries-old tradition that drew among others, the Emperor Jehangir; he records: "Fifteen times I went to look at Pushkar lake..."

Pilgrims bathe at any of the 52 *ghats* built around the three lakes of Pushkar called Senior, Middle and Junior or Bada, Manjhla and Chhota Pushkar respectively. Each *ghat*, each little waterbody is believed to be imbued with magical powers. Sombre-faced Brahmin priests lead the faithful to the Naga Kund or Serpent Lake — a dip here guarantees the production of a male heir, or so it is believed. The name 'Naga' in understandable for snakes are a recurring sexual image in many ancient cultures. A quick immersion to the accompaniment of a sacred chant at Kapil Vyapi Kund, named after the sage who lived in Vedic times, is alleged to be a sure cure for leprosy. Bathing at Roop Tirth (which transliterates roughly as Beauty Pilgrimage) promises instant beauty, while the Mrikand Muni Kund assures the gullible immediate and profound wisdom.

The continuous spectacle is of the village people dressed in their Sunday best and at their most ebullient. And why not? To them Pushkar is as much a place for religion as it is for some rumbunctious, good-natured frolic. Serious men and women buy and sell, barter and trade. Then, a sense of abandon takes over. Huge groups of women sing lustily and dance, exhorting diffident passers-by to come into their circle of joy. The men race camels and bullock carts or play tug-of-war with much whooping and back-thumping.

To others, Pushkar offers archaeological treasures inconspicuously tucked away in its myriad, cobbled streets. There is the 12th century Apteshwar Mahadeo temple dedicated to Shiva; also the Varaha temple which houses an image of Vishnu in his wild boar incarnation. Quite naturally, this votive image was found offensive by non-idolatrous Muslim conquerors: Jehangir in 1613 had orders issued for its prompt removal. His grandson Aurangzeb was so outraged that he destroyed the temple. The present statue was installed by a Rajput king only in 1784.

Another architecturally and historically

significant building is the 14th century Brahma temple. Aurangzeb ordered the smashing of the original idol in the 17th century. The idol was replaced, the temple extensively refurbished and the marble floors laid by a minister of the Maratha king, Daulat Ram Scindia, in the 19th century.

Above, and following pages: Vignettes from the annual camel fair at Pushkar.

THE PAINTED HOMES OF SHEKHAWATI

While the Raja (Birsinghdeo) was performing his duties in the Deccan, intelligence reached him that his son at home had usurped his title and authority; upon which, with only four horsemen, he left the army for his capital. When close to Khandela, he alighted at the house of a Jatni, of whom he requested refreshment, and begged especial care of his weary steed; lest he should be stolen; to which she sharply replied, "Is not Bahadur Singh ruler here? You may leave gold in the highway, and no one dare touch it". The old chieftain was so delighted with this testimony to his son's discharge of a prince's duties, that, without disclosing himself or his suspicions, he immediately returned to the Deccan, where he died.

— Col. James Tod

A dancer with a brass pot on her head framed in a window of the glittering Durbar Hall of Samode Palace close to Jaipur.

The story of Shekhawati in north-eastern Rajasthan, begins in the late 14th century with Bala, third son of Udaikaran, the powerful ruler of Amber. Rules of primogeniture precluded any prospect of attaining the eminence he yearned for, so Bala moved to nearby Barwada where he governed a small principality. Udaikaran allowed him to take away his favourite white mare upon condition that Bala would send a colt every year to Amber as a form of tribute, a subtle affirmation of his acknowledgement of Amber's suzerainty.

Bala's son, Mokul, unable to produce a male heir retired to Vrindavan where his guru suggested a three-pronged strategy guaranteed to produce results — he was to chant a secret incantation every day, pray to an idol of Gopinath (a manifestation of Krishna as lord of the milkmaids) and graze

Right: *This fresco painter's naivete is reflected in the depiction of the railway coach—a new-fangled invention he'd probably never seen. A railway carriage accommodates only two to four people.*
Facing page: *Kanwar Kesri Singh of Mandawa at Shekhawati waits stoically as two attendants tie a saffron, yellow and red 9-metre turban on his head.*

cows in pasture.

In the pastures, Mokul had a chance encounter with a blue-robed Muslim mystic, Sheikh Burhan, who promised him fulfilment of his desire upon condition that the new-born heir be bathed in cow's blood. In the fullness of time was born Shekha, the much-awaited royal heir, whose birth presented his father with a new dilemma, for how could a Hindu monarch bathe his baby in the blood of the holy cow? Quick thinking saved the

day, and the baby was bathed in goat's blood, while the colour of Sheikh Burhan's blue robe was adopted as that of the royal standard. The region itself is called Shekhawati, or the Garden of Shekha, after Shekha and the mystic whose spiritual powers brought him into being. The Vrindavan guru and his present of the auspicious Gopinath idol were not forgotten either, and Gopinath remains the presiding deity of the Shekhawats, as the Rajputs from this region style themselves.

Shekha attained only powerful local chieftain status, a fact ascribed to the use of goat's blood in bathing the royal infant, but managed to give nearby Amber many a sleepless night. He ascended the throne in 1445, and in a shrewd military move forged a political alliance with Pathan warriors from Gujarat, whom he persuaded to settle in his territory. Confident of his newly acquired military muscle, he threw the gauntlet at his titular sovereigns in Amber by refusing to send them the colt—the customary token of tribute and symbol of the Shekhawats' vassal status. Chandrasen of Amber rose to the bait and attacked his cousin. Shekha won the war and, along with it, a prefix and suffix to his name: henceforth his peers addressed him as Rao Shekhaji.

Shekhawati's subsequent history is about constant wars with Jaipur (where the Amber rulers had shifted) and the Muslim Kayamkhani nawabs of adjoining Fatehpur and Jhunjhunu, whom Shardul Singh defeated and expelled, ending their three-hundred-year-old supremacy in the region. Non-adherence to the rule of primogeniture led to large Shekhawat principalities being subdivided into pitifully small holdings, a development that marked the Shekhawats' forcible transition to lawless banditry as a means of survival. This confederation of irascible kinsmen whom the powerful rulers of Jaipur disliked as much as they dreaded were bribed with honours, but never trusted. The Shekhawats were denied permission to build mansions within the Jaipur city walls, all seven of whose formidable gates were closed upon them at dusk. In 1831 the British forced a treaty of accession on these proud people, who reluctantly agreed to acknowledge Jaipur's primacy. The treaty served British

Preceding page:
Shekhawati frescoes are an example of naive art as opposed to classical or folk art. Flying elephants on the border above are the only flights of fancy of an artist obviously moored in the miniature tradition as is reflected in the skewed perspective of this painting of a nobleman's procession.

interests by increasing contributions to Jaipur's revenue and their share of the same in direct proportion.

The enduring romance of Shekhawati today stems less from its colourful history and more from its ornate, jewel-like *havelis* that abound in a region where Marwari businessmen once conducted entrepôt trade. These *havelis* (the term, Persian in origin, connotes an enclosed place) were surrounded for reasons of safety and enclosed within for privacy, which was vital for women who lived in the seclusion of *purdah*. Here, within these intricately carved, profusely embellished structures, outer and inner courtyards demarcated the men's world from that of the women. Windows at three levels ensured a constant flow of warm air out of the upper storeys and the free inlet of cool air.

The art of fresco-buono, probably brought by the Mughals from Persia or introduced by European missionaries at Akbar's court, finds its most splendid expression on the façades and within the interiors of the *havelis* and palaces of this region. The Rajput was the first patron to commission artists to paint his forts, palaces and cenotaphs—but so was the merchant; the tradesman financed the ruler's campaigns, and the ornate *haveli* was the public announcement of his undeniable primacy and important status.

Shekhawati frescoes are 18th and 19th century images that provide insights into the growth and development of the people and the region. Traditional mythological deities such as Krishna in his various manifestations are repeatedly depicted. Recurring images of other deities give clues to the spiritual beliefs of these people. Ganesha was the auspicious elephant-headed god whose blessings were invoked at the commencement of any festival, marriage or journey — and the merchant made many long journeys. Lakshmi, the goddess of wealth, was an obvious, recurring votive image, for who else would the thrifty merchant, trading on small margins, worship? Representations of Indra, the rain-god, are an understandable inclusion in an area where the peasant laments in song that the meagre rain 'only wets one horn of his bullock, and not the other'.

The Shekhawati traders had to move out of the region with the opening of the seaports in Bombay and Calcutta, but returned ever so often to regale disbelieving country cousins with tales of wonderful modern inventions such as the camera, railway engine and motor car, all of which find the kind of clumsy figurative representation that could only have been the result of hearsay. At the Poddar *haveli* at Ramgarh, for instance, a carriage is just large enough to accommodate two full-size people; while one wall on a street in Mandawa depicts the mythological god Ram and his consort Sita descending in an aircraft.

British influence is increasingly evident in frescoes of the mid to late 19th century. Gold-worked lithographs had made their appearance at the Singhania *haveli* at Fatehpur, and these litho-and oleograph-inspired images are reflected in innumerable frescoes of the period. Portraits of white women with immodest necklines were not confined to the Rameshwar Lal Chaudhuri *haveli* in Fatehpur alone—*haveli* façades all over the region are splattered with similar images, marking a departure from earlier times, when only mythological female figures were depicted. Obviously, representations of 'loose' white women did not excite social approbation. Increased representation of European subjects — ladies walking poodles, gentlemen with guns, hats and wine bottles — reflected both the increased contact with and perception of an alien colonial master race.

Where else but in an impersonal fresco could the patron or artist record his myriad sexual fantasies? Thus erotica abounds: on the ceilings of the Mandawa fort a Rajput couple exchange passionate kisses; while other frescoes, as at the Ganeriwala *haveli* at Mukundgarh, depict couples in every conceivable sexual position.

Interestingly, many Hindu *havelis* in Fatehpur and elsewhere represent Muslim subjects: nawabs or the *barraq*, the mythical horse with a female head that carried Prophet Mohammed to heaven — features that reveal a secular sensibility. But frescoes on Muslim *havelis* in the same region remain confined to floral and geometric designs, and seem to consciously avoid figurative drawings that would be deemed anti-Islamic.

Samode, just outside Jaipur, has a comfortable palace hotel, but this was once a powerful state whose chief was prime minister of Jaipur. Apparently he embezzled enough state funds to build himself his impressive palace; its durbar hall has some fine *meenakari* (inlay of glass, mirror and semi-precious stones) work and a gilded ceiling that rivals that of the Jaipur maharaja's golden room in opulence. Sikar has the Biyani (a local merchant family) *havelis*, one of which is painted entirely in blue, a colour that was becoming increasingly popular in Europe.

Parsrampura is a revered settlement, for here lies the cenotaph of the illustrious Shardul Singh who drove the Muslim nawabs out of Shekhawati. Appropriately, the cenotaph commissioned by his wife commemorates his military prowess and is painted with scenes of Shardul in chain mail, marching at the head of an army composed of trains of elephants and sizeable battalions of fierce warriors in a medieval pageant replete with colour, costume and romance.

Nawalgarh's 18th century fort is now a granary, but contains within a painted dome with an exquisite aerial view of Jaipur. The façade of the Saat Haveli complex has a delightful mix of frescoes on a whole range of themes, from devotional to royal to company school (as the later mid-18th century frescoes influenced by modern British themes were termed). Here too is a Shiva temple with a multi-headed *lingam* and a building with marvellous early 19th century frescoes now sadly converted to a telephone exchange, its beautiful frescoes in danger of being obliterated by the streams of betel juice which are liberally expectorated on to ancient walls by nonchalant clerks.

En route to Mandawa is the mid-18th century fort of Dundlod that is now a palace hotel. Here, within medieval walls, lie rooms furnished with British four-poster beds, European chandeliers and porcelain bric-a-brac. The rulers' frescoed palace has its counterpoint in the lavishly embellished Goenka merchant *haveli* whose rooms glow with frescoes on the Radha-Krishna theme. Nearby Laxmangarh, with its Char-chowk (four-courtyard) *haveli*, is an interesting destination. The fort has a spectacular view of the city, with neat streets laid at right angles and wide squares that evoke memories of Jaipur. This is no mere coincidence—Laxmangarh was the only city in this area planned after the Jaipur model.

Step into the wide courtyard of Castle Mandawa, and you could be in another, historic world. A brass gong, startlingly loud in the stillness of the desert, sounds the hour, and echoes resound within 18th century walls where time seems to stand still. Wander through the precincts of the *zenana*, now converted into comfortable hotel rooms; in the adjoining museum, gaze in wonder at satin and brocade standards carried into war by Rajput warriors; marvel at the richness and variety of ceremonial headgear and costumes on display. In a quaint juxtaposition of 'beauty' with the 'beast', handles made of jade and gold enamel cap cruel weapons.

Ramayana retold a la Shekhawati—Lakshman drives his brother Lord Rama and his wife Sita home in a Rolls Royce.

Ramgarh, near Mandawa, houses the domed cenotaph of local business baron Poddar, which has the Ramayana in frescoes on its walls. A detour to Mehansar takes one to the Sone Chandi ki Haveli (gold and silver mansion) and into the most exquisite golden room in the region. Once a jeweller's showroom, it still dazzles the eye with its gilded ceiling, frescoed walls, European cut-glass chandeliers, Belgian mirrors in gilt frames, and lithos of half-clad European ladies.

Today, the Shekhawati's mansions stand forlorn and deserted. The neglect of such monuments might seem stupefying, unless looked at in perspective: this is a civilisation whose inhabitants have internalised eternal concepts of the transience and evanescense of all things, including life itself. Such a people would preserve those of gods; the abodes of men inspire much less respect.

THE HUNT

"COME AND STAY WITH US IN INDIA AND WE will arrange for you to shoot tigers from the backs of elephants or elephants from the backs of tigers", Lord Curzon, when India's Viceroy, boasted in a letter to a friend in England. He was undoubtedly talking about the royal game reserves of Rajasthan, where local princes made it a point to honour their guests with a successful hunt, arranging special safaris with beaters for big cats. Here, royal guests would `rough it out' in carpeted tents with brick floors, fireplaces, dressing rooms and alfresco drawing rooms complete with Persian rugs—and, of course, gourmet meals washed down with a constant supply of champagne, beer, hock, brandy and liqueurs; Rolls Royce and Buick safaris waited on call.

The princes understood Purdy Politics well and were keenly aware that nothing projected them in a more favourable light than a successful shoot in their territory. No subterfuge was too big to feed the fragile British ego. Thus, special tape measures were devised to give flattering estimates of the slain tiger's size— "never less than ten feet for the Viceroy". If the Viceroy was a lousy marksman, beaters were quietly instructed to gather a sizeable group of birds shot by the rest of the party and place them in a flattering pile at the imperial feet for the commemorative photograph.

This combination of royal politics and passion for the hunt almost decimated the wildlife population of the region. It was perfectly normal for 4,000 sand grouse to be downed on a particular morning at Bikaner. Lord Linlithgow presided as guest of honour at the massacre of 4,273 birds at Bharatpur in 1938. Between the turn of the century and 1971, when the killing of tigers was outlawed, the maharajas, with some help from their British friends, had managed to put away almost 39,000 of these cats. Dholpur was in the habit of shooting a tiger before breakfast; the seemingly will o' the wisp Maharani Gayatri Devi of Jaipur bagged 27; Olympic marksman and sharpshooter Dr. Karni Singh of Bikaner had put away almost 50 before he turned conservationist ... as Lady Birdwood, daughter of an Udaipur Resident at the turn of the century remarked wryly, "My dear, they shot everything that moved or flew!"

Today, the erstwhile royal hunting grounds are tranquil sanctuaries where tigers roam free. A dazzling variety of birds and waterfowl delight the ornithologist's eye. In the heart of the forest you may sight herds of deer, antelope, blackbuck or blue bulls.

The Keoladeo Ghana sanctuary, which gets its name from the Keoladeo temple of Lord Shiva, is 11 sq miles of freshwater marshland, created at the confluence of the Ban-Ganga and Ruparel rivers by Maharaja Kishen Singh of Bharatpur at the turn of the century. Kishen Singh had savoured the buck-shooting spots of England and decided to create one for himself. To attract birds to Bharatpur, he had a forest flooded with water from the Ganbir river during the rainy season. Next, he had it drained out so that the lowlands remained filled with water. Muddy butts with shady trees were created to facilitate duck shoots. Lord Kitchener and Lord Curzon were invited for the inaugural massacre in 1902. The Prince of Wales came with his party for a second time in 1922, and shot 2,221 birds. Over the years Bharatpur's guest list included royalty from neighbouring states as well as faraway Afghanistan, Malaysia and Iran. The last ruler gifted it to the Rajasthan government, and Keoladeo Ghana reserve became a sanctuary in 1956.

Today the Bharatpur sanctuary, as it is also called, is home to almost 350 species of birds. The extraordinary variety of flora provides convenient nesting places, while the lakes, with their algae, aquatic grasses and flowering plants, provide food and cover to amphibians, fish and insects, upon which the birds depend for raising their young.

In the surrounding scrubland you could walk or take a rough ride in a rickshaw along the raised embankments, from where you can spot blue bulls, wild boar, feral cattle, civets and small jungle cats. There's a certain magic in waking up at the crack of dawn to the sound of a thousand birds and walking through early morning mist to catch sight of the brilliant desert sun breaking through a lilac-pink sky.

Ranthambore, nestling between the Aravalli and Vindhya mountain ranges and situated a convenient eleven kilometres from Sawai Madhopur railway station, was once the shooting preserve of the Jaipur maharajas; today it is one of India's conservation success stories. Ranthambore was taken up under Project Tiger in 1973 in an effort to preserve a species that was in danger of extinction. There were 14 tigers here in 1973 — at last count there were 40, and these are so obviously secure in their habitat that they make diurnal as well as nocturnal appearances. The animals' habitat is lush, emerald green forest, seasonally set ablaze with the fiery red blossoms of thousands of *dhak* trees. Deep in the forest monkeys hoot in alarm and set off a cacophony of anxious bird-calls even as a tigress bellows for her wandering cubs from some dank mountain recess. Herds of spotted deer streak past in a brown-and-silver flash. Your guide halts the jeep, raises a finger to his lips, and you turn around slowly, hackles rising, to gaze, mesmerised, into the cold, glittering eyes of a magnificent tiger. Elsewhere, giant monitor lizards suddenly spring into view and change into all the colours of the rainbow in front of your disbelieving eyes. Sitting under the enormous 'walking' banyan tree that flanks the Jogi Mahal resthouse within the sanctuary, hearing the panoply of strange bird-calls at twilight, you will experience the compelling, hypnotic appeal of the forest.

Overhead looms the brooding fort of Ranthambore with ramparts that extend seven kilometres long. This was the Rajput stronghold that fell to the mighty Delhi Sultan Ala-ud-din-Khilji in 1303. At that time 20,000 women committed *jauhar*, an event repeated in 1569 when the Mughal emperor Akbar stormed the fort.

Sariska, also close to Jaipur, which is twice the size of Ranthambore, was the hunting ground of the Alwar maharaja. In this 800 sq mile-area are forested valleys and jagged hills that soften with flame trees in spring but are sere and brown in summer and windy and harsh in winter, when birds from Siberia and China flock here to seek refuge from sub-zero temperatures. Wild boar, blue bulls, jackals, scavengers, leopards, chital and sambar flock to natural waterholes; forest authorities have also created artificial waterbodies to provide succour during the intense summer heat. Rhesus monkeys, langurs and blue bulls are more easily viewed than leopards, who are a very elusive sight at this forest retreat; but then, patience is of the essence in the forest. The turn-of-the-century Sariska Palace hotel, the Alwar maharaja's private residence, is where the old royal hunting parties would repose in eau-de-cologned, Vichy water comfort after the bi-annual massacres that were as much 'society' as safari affairs.

A pleasant drive away is the picturesque lakeside royal hunting lodge of Siliserh, now run as a hotel by the tourist authorities. Rajorgarh, the third-century Gurjar-Pratihara capital, is to Alwar what Amber is to Jaipur. This was where Alwar's Pratap Singh built his 18th century fortress on the ruins of the ancient one. Devastated old gardens and monuments offer mute testimony to the erstwhile capital's grandeur. A little into the interior of the sanctuary is the medieval hilltop fortress of Kankwari that has a spectacular terrace view and some marvellously well-preserved frescoes within its crumbling apartments.

The Desert National Park, 45 km southwest of Jaisalmer, is no soothing, vernal retreat. Vegetation is sparse in this sprawling, 1,220 sq mile territory, where survival is a struggle for the scant flora and fauna that are found here. Temperatures careen from sub-zero to 130° F, but the hardy desert fox and the intimidating desert rat thrive. Wolves, jackals, blackbuck and blue bulls co-exist with crested porcupines and exotic desert birds like the Indian bustard, shrikes, flycatchers, bee-eaters and the magnificent sand grouse, who descend in turbulent flocks on the meagre waterholes. Huge populations of blackbuck live in this area, a fact ascribed to the presence of large Bishnoi settlements in the vicinity. These tribes believe that the souls of their ancestors dwell in these animals, and it is from such simple belief that a conservation ethic was inculcated in this community.

At Akal, 14 km from Jaisalmer, is the curious Wood Fossil Park where ancient, gnarled tree stumps date back a hundred and eighty million years. In geological terms they belong to the Lower Jurassic age in the Mesozoic era, when the earth was passing through its middle stage of development. This was once hot and humid land with large freshwater lakes and dense vegetation. In this steamy, swampy plain thrived strange plants like cycads—bizarre hybrids of ferns and palms—which grew along with even more exotic species of plants and mosses. Today you may see the fossils of plants and trees of an age when dinosaurs roamed this very region.

Hunting trophies after a shoot at Alwar. Game was regularly decimated by royal hunting parties, but there was a streak towards conservation too, for the hunting preserves were meant only for royal shikar.

CITIES OF THE DESERT

We came to sand-hills, which at first were covered with bushes, but afterwards were naked piles of loose sand, rising one after another like the waves of the sea, and marked on the surface by the wind like drifted snow. There were roads through them, made solid by the treading of animals; but off the road are horses sunk into the sand above the knee.
— Marquis of Elphinstone, 1808

Maharaja Gaj Singh of Jodhpur in royal regalia in the gilded Phool Mahal Palace at Mehrangarh fort. In the foreground is the octagonal throne of the Jodhpur rulers.

incestuous relationship between the Rajput vassal and his Mughal suzerain.

The durbar hall or Phool Mahal, overlooking the Daulat Khana Chowk, with its gilded ceiling, stained glass windows, profusion of painted wall panels and two Belgian glass mirrors between which sits a golden wooden throne is an appropriate setting for a king. The profusion of *jalis* on the Jhanki Mahal of the *zenana* gives the façade of sym-

Women sit in their natural habitat —their huts plastered with a mix of cowdung and earth.

metrical windows capped by bangladhar eaves the appearance of a piece of hanging lace: an incredible feat, considering the heavy stone medium. The entire façade of the upper storeys is corbelled out to overhang the supporting ground storey, with stunning effect.

The Mardana Deori has an exquisite display of Jodhpur miniatures, including some amusing ones of opium-eaters skittering away in fright from a big black rat, and an unusual depiction of the royal ladies playing polo. Portraits of Raja Mansingh abound — this eccentric ruler's spiritual pendulum swung from frenzied religiosity to frenetic sensuality, and his alleged hobby prior to his transition to a chaster frame of mind was composing bawdy couplets about everyone ranging from his courtiers to his mother-in-law! Not only Jodhpur riches, but also loot from various campaigns is on display: a velvet brocade Mughal tent and a gilded glass palanquin wrested from Buland Khan of Ahmedabad by Maharaja Abhay Singh. There is also a display of armoury, ancient manuscripts and the incredible range of turbans of this region.

On another part of the hill is Jaswant Thada, a 19th century cenotaph built to honour Jaswant Singh. While all Jodhpur rulers have their cenotaphs at Mandore, this maharaja's *chhatri*, built in 1899 of marble mined from Makrana, was commissioned here by his widow. This is a serene monument with marble walls, so translucent that light can penetrate into the structure even though it has no windows.

Umaid Bhawan Palace is an exercise in Rathore rococo translated into a concrete pink-sandstone, 347-room reality by H.V. Lancaster, whose earlier experience of working with Edward Lutyens and erecting municipal buildings in his native England is amply mirrored in this structure that closely resembles a town hall converted into a formal country estate. This was Maharaja Umaid Singh's famine relief project for the Jodhpur peasantry, three thousand of whom worked for fifteen years to complete this building, and whose grandeur has more to do with scale than design. A special railway line carried sandstone 10 km to a site with no water for the construction of a building that had among the first lifts and airconditioning systems introduced in Indian palaces of that era. Other attractions include a banquet hall for three hundred, a private auditorium, a spectacular double-domed ceiling with a whispering gallery and a la mode art-deco paintings by the visiting Polish artist Norblin. The furniture was a disaster, for the ship carrying the specially ordered suites sank, while the factory in London from which it was subsequently re-ordered was bombed during the

German blitzkreig. The result: an Indo-Rajput palace with art-deco artefacts and ponderous country house furniture. Today it is a palace hotel which doubles as a royal residence and also houses a charming museum with a collection of quaint old watches and alarm clocks, porcelain bric-a-brac and old royal dinner-party menus that give vital clues to the inclinations of royal and viceregal palates.

Jodhpur has other delights to offer, like the Ram Rasoda or community kitchen in the heart of its old *bazar*, where destitutes are still fed by Jain merchants. There are the Kunj Behari and Chamunda temples on the banks of the Gulab Sagar lake, mentioned by Colonel Tod as being famous for its pomegranates, once exported to other regions. The temple of the Nath Sampradaya sect, of which Raja Mansingh was a follower, is tucked away in a quiet bylane of the old city.

Jodhpur's markets in narrow, cobbled streets, bustling with camels and urchins and lined with old *havelis*, offer unexpected delights. Rainbow coloured tie and dye fabric, handcrafted shoes, called *jootis*, or the famous Jodhpur breeches. In the Sardar market with its distinctly medieval air stroll the inhabitants of the desert in vibrant reds, sensuous saffrons and *electric blues* that defy rather than deflect the heat and mirror their wild and colourful temperament. These are not a people who have succumbed—they have survived the desert and conquered it, for in this land of death, the impulse to life and all its beauty endures.

Mandore, a short drive from Jodhpur, has an air of seclusion befitting a kingdom eclipsed by history. Appropriately, cenotaphs of once-mighty kings and their fragile consorts are the only surviving monuments. The memorials to Jaswant Singh and Ajit Singh are expecially distinctive the first for sheer scale, the other for symmetry of design. *Satis* consumed by fires of fidelity too have monuments consecrated to their memories. The Hall of Heroes, carved on a single rockface is neither architecturally nor aesthetically pleasingly with its giant, extremely naive sculptural renditions of folk heroes.

At Osian, an erstwhile trading centre of the Jains, 65 km from Jodhpur, prosperous traders built spectacular temples to their deities: these include the 12th century Sachiya Mata temple, profusely embellished within and without, and reached through a sandstone arch carved with celestial nymphs. Nagaur, 135 km from Jodhpur, was once the stronghold of the Naga Rajputs and the home town of Sheikh Abul Fazal, the celebrated historian of Akbar's court. Within the formidable hillside fort are mosques and jet fountains built by Shah Jahan and Akbar and an

inscription by the Hindu raja, Mansingh, that reads: 'Whoever rules this town, whether Hindu or Muslim, must protect this mosque.'

A careless insinuation, a thoughtless witticism, a fancied slight, an injured ego — such was the genesis of the medieval kingdom of Bikaner. Rao Bika was the second son of Rao Jodha of

Mud-plastered floors are sprinkled with water on hot days. A natural consequence is a cooling effect and increased hardening over successful dousings.

Top: *When Mehrangarh fort was completed in 1459, in continuance of a ghoulish tradition, the architect Bambhi Rajra was said to have been buried alive with its defence secrets.*

Above: *The white marble pavilion marks a distinct change of pace from the ponderous municipal-style architectural form imposed on Umaid Bhavan palace by its architect.*

Jodhpur; piqued at a quiet aside the younger son was exchanging with his uncle Kandhal in the royal court, Jodha asked the duo whether they were planning a conspiracy against him. An indignant Bika, cut to the quick, strode out of the court and his father's kingdom, determined to earn his respect and find his fortune. Find it he did, at the expense of the Godara Jats, whose territories he annexed with his ragtag band of three hundred followers. It was an appropriate moment for conquest—the Godaras were weary from combating the Bhatti raiders' periodic incursions into their territory, and welcomed a

settler suzerain. The year was 1486.

Shrewd military and political manoeuvrings, sealed by the inevitable matrimonial alliance, ensured the fledgling kingdom's rise to enviable eminence: by the 16th century, Emperor Jahangir broke from the formalese characteristic of the Mughal *firmans* to address Rao Sur Singh as an equal: "Raoji, please receive our Ram Ram". (His Turkish great-grandfather would have been appalled.) Raids by Bhatti neighbours and Rathore cousins were effectively repelled; revenue from levies on caravans was carefully husbanded; by 1587, Rao Rai Singh had started building the Junagarh Fort, and a city flowered in the midst of desolation.

Often attacked but never conquered, Junagarh held within its ramparts 37 palaces, pavilions and temples in a palimpsest created almost continuously upto the early 20th century. Apartments were decorated in the Mughal style by successive kings who sought to emulate the splendours of the Delhi court, making up with ingenuity what they lacked in resource, and achieving remarkably similar effects. A superb example of this triumph is the coronation room in Anup Mahal, where

the profusion of red and gold gives the impression of expensive pietra dura, while it is in fact a marvel of gold paint and lacquer used to create an illusion of extravagance.

The play of illusion and reality continues in Badal Mahal, which has images of rain clouds painted on walls so that royal siblings would not forget the smells and sounds of a monsoon that was always a fickle visitor in these regions. A huge European-style portrait, the work of a visiting Italian artist, depicts a Shekhawati chieftain meeting a Bikaner chief, each immediately identified by his distinctive turban. Elsewhere in the complex, lime plaster and ground marble have been used to achieve the effect of marble. Har Mandir, where the royals still celebrate births and weddings, has a finely-crafted idol of Navdurga seated on a nine-petalled gold lotus. Gaj Mandir is a mirror palace complete with an ivory-inlaid bed and ornate silver chairs, named after the legendary Gaj Singh, father of 61 sons, all but six of whom, as Colonel Tod puts it with endearing Victorian delicacy, were 'sons of love'.

Today, the fort is a museum: here can be seen Rao Bika's small, silver-legged bed; the

ancient sandalwood throne of the Kanauj kings; the screened corridors of the *zenana* apartments; or the vastly amusing little chamber under the bright blue clock tower where Dutch tiles are juxtaposed against Rajput miniatures on Chinese wallpaper. The Maharaja Ganga Singh durbar hall bristles with a display of armaments: sly knives that fanned into multi-pointed weapons of destruction within the assailed body; crafty little pistol daggers; wings of WWI fighter planes.

Lallgarh succeeds where Jodhpur's Umaid Bhawan does not, for this red sandstone Swinton Jacob building which is today

Top: The exterior façade of palace apartments within Junagarh — a fort within which rulers added apartments continuously for over 400 years.
Above: The red sandstone Lallgarh Palace is an imposing turn-of-the-century monument. The façade is Oriental, the decor within Occidental, but the cross-cultural blend is surprisingly successful.

Preceding page: Women throng the Mehrangarh courtyard which remained verboten to the royal ladies for centuries.

a palace-hotel represents a successful blending of Renaissance style with traditional Rajput architectural form. The oriental façade, with its profusion of pavilion-kiosks, finely carved balconies and balustrades, merges with its occidental interiors, profusely embellished with Belgian and Bohemian glass crystal chandeliers. Here are billiards, card and smoking rooms linked with corridors, lined with old lithographs and hunting tro-

The early-20th century Durbar Hall at Junagarh built by Maharaja Ganga Singh. The motifs carved on the stone walls below are echoed on the wooden arches above.

phies, evoking the ambience of quieter, more spacious times. In another part of the palace, the magnificient manuscript collection of the 17th century scholar-king Anup Singh is housed in a library that bears his name.

Within the city are the 14th century Jain temples of Bhandeshwar and Sandeshwar, noteworthy for their frescoes and stylised gold-leaf wall paintings. Old Jain *havelis* such as those of the Khajanchis and the Kotharis can be visited by prior appointment. The opulent interiors are replete with eclectic, if whimsical, art collections; furniture that is a startling mix of Birmingham and Bombay, and an abundance of lacy balustrades, carved sandalwood doors and windows.

Close by is Gajner, the erstwhile hunting lodge of the maharaja, scene of the fabled annual sand grouse shoot hosted by Maharaja Ganga Singh, an invitation to which was shamelessly coveted by Indian princes and successive British viceroys. Ganga Singh was the modern monarch who brought in the railways and the Ganga canal and mined coal so profitably as to treble his state's revenue. The shoot was an exercise in diplomacy that helped achieve the maharaja's objectives—he got British sanction for the Gang Canal which brought water to his parched land.

At Deshnoke, 32 km away, stands the temple of Karni Mata, a mystic worshipped as a reincarnation of Durga in her own lifetime, who blessed young Rao Bika and prophesied his victory. Here, not the mother goddess alone, but the well-fed rats, called kabas, whose bodies are believed to house the souls of her departed devotees, receive the respectful homage of millions. The entrance to the temple is through a carved marble arch leading to a black and white marble courtyard topped by a wire mesh which protects the rats from eagles, crows and hawks. Whosoever, howsoever innocently tramples upon these divine rodents must present a gold or silver replica to the temple or saffer ghastly misfortune. Less credulous defaulters may, however, suffer no more than a mild attack of conservation ethic inspired guilt! Closed to Bikaner is Devikundsagar, where a group of cenotaphs are built around an artificial tank. Memorials carved with suns denote the resting places of princes; those marked with tiny lotus flowers commemorate princesses.

The last word on any place or people is ultimately that of the traveller, and is often a matter of perspective. Witness these diametrically opposed contemporaneous accounts of two turn-of-the century European travellers. One waxes eloquent: "In Bikaner today you see so much silk that you really wonder if this is jangal country, or not rather Kashmir. Everywhere beautiful women full of grace and modesty, everywhere fierce warriors used to handle the sword..." The other is downright sniffy: "The people of Bikaner are exceedingly dirty, both in their persons and habits"!!! Opinions change, as men often do, Bikaner, however, endures.

PALATIAL LIFESTYLES

IT IS STILL POSSIBLE TO LIVE LIKE A PRINCE IN the middle of the desert in India. At Mandawa Palace in Shekhawati you can eat an eight course meal on the huge terrace while liveried retainers watch over you, spears in hand to keep away marauding eagles. At nearby Dundlod you could sleep on a brass four - poster bed and dine off Wedgwood porcelain in a room crammed with colonial furniture. It is the quaint juxtaposition that charms: the mulligatawny soup that precedes dinner is authentic Indo-British, the light lemon souffle that follows would do a French chef proud! The Piramal mansion at Bagar has been lovingly restored, its marble corridors and spacious high ceilinged rooms have a distinct turn of the century flavour

En route from Jodhpur to Udaipur lies the marble palace of Ghanerao, its luxurious façade sadly limewashed over by the father of the present Thakur Sajjan Singh. Evidence of the original splendour lingers in the marble *baradari* on the first floor. The nobleman's English-speaking wife still lives in strict *purdah* in this castle that has a magnificent view of Kumbhalgarh fort. The meals are simple, the rooms almost spartan, but history comes alive here in the sepia-tinted portraits of family weddings and celebrations that form part of the decor.

Neemrana on the Delhi-Jaipur highway is evidence of the triumph of mind over matter. This 15th century fort abandoned to bats and wild bushes has been restored with great attention to detail by a French businessman turned Indophile and his poet-partner. In the process of renovation, the duo have managed to revive the lost art of *araish*, the process whereby lime surfaces are polished to resemble marble as also the tradition of fine stone carving. Delicate *jharokas* (filigreed window screens) chiselled by descendants of the geniuses who probably made the originals,

tastefully furnished interiors and a terrace with a view of made-to-order sunsets constitute the romance that is Neemrana.

Then there are the sumptuous hunting lodges turned hotels tucked away in remote forests as in Sariska near Alwar, Sawai Madhopur and Ramgarh near Jaipur, and Gajner close to Bikaner. Sariska Palace's majestic façade is now smothered in pistachio and yellow paint, but some of the old charm glimmers through in the cool, airy rooms and the sweeping lawns. Ramgarh, closer to Jaipur, has larger suites, Liberty-print furnishings and stunning views of the lake.

And to think that Rambagh Palace could have been the property of a housemaid! Raja Ram Singh had gifted the place in the 19th century to Kesar Badaran, his Rewa queen's chief attendant. Mercifully, the property reverted to the royals by virtue of the law of escheat. Custom-made carpets, lotus-leaf marble fountains, Lalique glass furniture and a handsome Polo Bar with an indoor fountain constitute this popular palace hotel's unique appeal. Raj Mahal and Jai Mahal have their own quiet beauty.

No mention of palace hotels would be complete without referece to the lakeside Shiv Niwas palace or the legendary Lake Palace of Udaipur. These are opulent retreats. The lotus arches, frescoed stained glass interiors furnished with Lalique and silver furniture are the very stuff of oriental fantasy.

Narain Niwas, Jaipur: the townhouse of the aristocratic Kanota family is now a popular hotel in the state capital.

THE POWER AND THE GLORY OF UDAIPUR

It was in Bhagwat Singh's time that Queen Elizabeth II paid a visit to Udaipur and was received as a guest at Shiv Niwas. When he naturally offered the Queen precedence, she demurred, saying, "Please lead the way. You come from a much older family than I do!"
— Brian Masters

Palace attendants in Udaipur tying cummerbunds in preparation for a ceremonial occasion. In their hand they hold the imperial canopy, royal standards and a chamar made of yak's tail.

Top: The temple of Charbhujaji near Udaipur where Vishnu is depicted in a martial stance.
Above: Details from the Peacock Courtyard in the City Palace in Udaipur.

It was an accident of history that led to the foundation of the dynasty of the Sisodias, uninterrupted rulers for the course of a stupendous fourteen hundred years of the premier Hindu kingdom of Mewar, whose boundaries once stretched all the way from coastal Gujarat to distant Ajmer. This was the clan which ruled for almost eight centuries from the awesome medieval rock fort of Chittor, built the intimidating Kumbhalgarh whose enormous fortified walls seemed "more the works of giants than men" to the incredulous 19th century historian, Colonel Tod, and which, together with these ruggedly masculine edifices, was also responsible for the achingly beautiful, delicate lakeside city called Udaipur.

The founding of this mighty dynasty goes back to the sixth century, when the pregnant queen Pushpavati of Vallabhi in Gujarat made her arduous journey to the northern Aravallis on a pilgrimage to pray for the well-being of her unborn child. The Vallabhi kings had ruled for four centuries, after having migrated from their early stronghold on the borders of Kashmir. The family claimed illustrious descent as progeny of Luv, elder of the twin sons of Ram. It was in the remote, mountainous Aravallis that news reached Pushpavati of the destruction of Vallabhi and the death of her husband at the hands of unknown invaders from the west. Stoic in her grief, the queen retreated to a hillside cave to await the birth of the royal heir who would ensure the continuation of his father's dynasty.

In the fullness of time was born a child she named Guhil. Dry-eyed, she rose from her natal bed, entrusted the infant to her maid's care, ordered a funeral pyre lit and walked into it to join her dead husband's soul. Guhil grew up among the Bhils, the ancient tribal inhabitants of the Aravallis. As he played one day, a Bhil playmate cut his own thumb with a sword and smeared the blood on Guhil's forehead. The Bhils — a simple hill people — interpreted this as a divine portent and anointed young Guhil as their ruler. His descendants were the Guhilots, who established kingdoms at nearby Nagda before moving in the seventh century to the Mewar plains. En route they encamped briefly at a village called Sisodia and from then on styled themselves as Sisodias.

The eighth-century Bappa Rawal wrested Chittor, the craggy fort atop a steep mountain, from the Mori rulers, and it was here that his Sisodia descendants ruled for almost eight centuries till 1567, when Akbar devastated their stronghold after a long and vicious siege. The Sisodias and their kingdom were the most prominent and enduring symbol of Hindu valour and military might; in effecting their subjugation, the Muslim invaders made a significant political and military point to other Hindu kingdoms not inclined to accept their suzerainty.

Akbar's was a pyrrhic victory. He entered to take possession of a charred, smoking ruin, not the ornate mountain palace he had so long coveted. There were no prisoners of war to fetter and humiliate in public parades, no women to carry off in concubinage to the royal harems. Thirty thousand Rajputs laid down their lives rather than sacrifice their freedom. In a smouldering field of ash lay the scorched remains of nine Sisodia queens, five princesses and hundreds of women and children of Rajput noblemen who had preferred death to dishonour.

This was not the first such holocaust to visit Chittor. As early as 1303, Allauddin Khilji the Tartar had attacked the fort, agreeing to lift the protracted siege only on the condition that he be allowed a view of the ravishing Padmini, wife of the regent of Chittor, Rana Ratan Singh. The Rajputs reluctantly agreed when it was suggested that the invader satisfy himself with just a glimpse of the queen in a mirror. Padmini descended the steps of a poolside pavilion, but when Allauddin Khilji saw her reflection in the limpid waters, he immediately decided on a treacherous volte-face — she was a worthy prize indeed! The Rana, in time-honoured tradition, escorted his guest to the entrance gate where, upon a signal from the Sultan, his men rushed in to ambush Ratan Singh. Allauddin Khilji then demanded the surrender of Padmini as the price of the Rana's release. To his delighted surprise she agreed, and came to his camp with an entourage of lady attendants in a whole line of screened palanquins. What emerged to greet him, however, were not the *zenana* ladies but fierce Rajput warriors, who slew his guards, rescued their Rana and queen and swept up the hill to the fortress.

The enraged Sultan mounted a savage attack to avenge his humiliation; within the fort, queens, princesses, noblewomen and children attired in their traditional finery calmly prepared for the rite of *jauhar*. "The funeral pyre was lighted within the great subterranean retreat in chambers impervious to the light of day, and the defenders of Chittor beheld in procession the queens, their own wives and daughters, to the number of several thousands. The fair Padmini closed the throng ... They were conveyed to the cavern and the opening closed upon them". The Rajput braves, eyes glazed with opium, heads smeared with the ashes of their women and children, donned saffron robes — the colour of martyrdom — and rushed out to slay as many of the invaders as possible before being slain...

It was a scenario that was to repeat itself in 1534 when Bahadur Shah of Gujarat, lured by Chittor's recently discovered silver mines, attacked the kingdom. The widow of the Rana, Rani Karnavati calmly led 13,000 women into the *jauhar* ceremony even as thirty-two thousand warriors died fighting to a man in the last desperate charge.

Such was the brave history of the kingdom that was inherited by Rana Kumbha who in turn forged the erstwhile fissiparous Rajput kingdoms into a fearsome Hindu confederation and with his phalanx of a hundred-thousand archers and horsemen and fourteen hundred elephants inflicted a humiliating defeat on the sultan of Malwa. He alone built thirty-two of the eighty four mighty

Below and bottom: Interiors of Shiv Niwas Palace and Lake Palace, Udaipur. Planned as royal retreats for the summer months, both are now luxurious hotels.

69

Miniatures depicting the Geet Govinda with Krishna as its principal character, from the Government Museum in Udaipur. These originals date from the 18th century.

forts of Mewar. His grandson, Rana Sangram Singh was the fabled Rana Sanga, a veteran of innumerable wars whose armies had intimidated Akbar's grandfather, Babur, in the decisive battle of Khanua in 1527 and to whom, but for a fortunate twist of fate, Babur would certainly have lost the war.

Following Akbar's siege over Chittor, Rana Udai Singh II moved to the relative safety of the defensive retreat of Udaipur that ultimately became the new Sisodia capital and was quiescent enough, but his son Maharana Pratap (1572-1597) remained a continuous thorn in the flesh for Akbar for the next quarter century. His imperial forces waged relentless guerilla warfare on the Mughals and the Rana Pratap lived up to his promise that he would never eat off solid utensils or sleep on a bed or under a roof till he had recovered Chittor — a dream he could tragically never realise. Akbar respected Rana Pratap as much as he feared him but failed to break or befriend this lion of the desert in his lifetime. Twenty-seven kilometres from Udaipur is the narrow pass of Haldighati where the implacable foes last met. The Mughal forces failed to vanquish Rana Pratap

who was ambushed thrice but galloped away on his legendary steed, Chetak; the wounded horse died after reaching his master to safety and a memorial to Chetak stands at the spot where he fell.

Rana Amar Singh (1597 - 1620) fought seventeen pitched battles with Emperor Jehangir, Akbar's son, before finally agreeing to an honorable peace whereby the Mughals tacitly agreed to abide by their staunch refusal to send a Sisodia princess to the Mughal bed. Chittor too was restored upon condition that Amar Singh was not to attempt to fortify it again. Even on such honorable terms the accord with an outside power depressed Amar Singh so much that he never emerged from his city palace at Udaipur. This abhorrence of 'foreign authority', of anything that they constituted as 'interference', was a leifmotif in Udaipur. As late as the 20th century the feisty Maharana Fateh Singh refused to set up a finance department, leave alone initiate plans of commercial or agricultural improvement at the British Resident's behest. "I am Rajput," he snubbed him in a reflex that seemed almost genetic, "soldier and statesman. Not tradesman". The British

representative of the 'nation of shopkeepers' had to swallow the insult!

Chittor today still inspires awe. This fine example of medieval Hindu defence architecture soars 500 feet into the sky. At the entrance is the Bhairon Pol with memorials to Jaimal of Badnore and Patta of Kelwa, teenage Rathore heroes of the siege of 1567. Immortalised in balladeers songs, Jaimal was killed by Akbar himself while Patta, dressed in saffron, together with his mother and young wife died fighting in the final charge. An impressed Akbar erected memorials to these heroes in his fort at Agra. Within the sprawling fort of Chittor is the tranquil poolside palace of Rani Padmini, the impressive 15th century Kumbha Shyama temple dedicated to Lord Vishnu, the 16th century temple of the legendary Krishna devotee queen Mirabai —daughter-in-law of Rana Sanga, and the 120 feet high, nine-storeyed Vijay Stambha built by Rana Kumbha to commemorate his victory over the Sultan of Malwa. This remarkably well preserved limestone structure connected by a winding staircase is smothered with intricate carvings depicting social and religious themes, a tribute to Hindu tol-

erance and cultural catholicity, built to commemorate a Hindu king's victory over a Muslim potentate with the name of 'Allah' in Arabic script. A smaller, exquisitely carved tower is Kirti Stambh built in honour of the first Jain *tirthankara*, Adinath. Rana Kumbha's palace is a perfect example of a royal Hindu complex — stables lead to guard houses that lead to a *durbar* court and deep within its recesses are the private apartments. Hindu embellishments like elephant and lotus motifs, multi-storeyed balconies and terraces contribute to its distinct ambience. Today vultures roam and wolves bay in palaces once resonant with the sound of music, and the tinkle of silver anklets.

Kumbhalgarh, two hours north of Udaipur, is the 15th century fort built by Rana Kumbha. A bend on a steep mountain road reveals a sight that makes one almost stumble in shock — on a rock peak 3,500 feet high are serpentime, undulating walls twenty feet thick that stretch across a span of thirty-two kilometers. Kumbha built his hilltop fort on the site of an earlier 2nd century Jain edifice after winning it from the Mer ruler who offered himself as sacrifice to strengthen

Following page: The 17th century Jag Niwas is today known as the Lake Palace—one of the most romantic hotel resorts in the world. The property spans four acres—within lie marble-floored, granite-tiled pavilions and lavishly-decorated rooms built around gardens and fountains. At the lakeside is the City Palace, now converted into the Shiv Niwas Hotel.

its foundations. Within the crenallated ramparts is a twelve kilometre enclosure dotted with palaces, temples, stables, residences for royal attendants, water resources, farms, kitchen gardens — everything needed to withstand a long siege. Kumbhalgarh fell but only to the combined might of the Mughal, Amber and Marwar forces. They could not breach the defences and only won by infecting the fort's water supply source. The im-

Maharana Mahendra Singh of Udaipur, his wife and son, flank his newly-wed daughter and son-in-law at a private function.

Fort and battlements of Chittorgarh—seat of the Sisodia Rajputs for 800 years before they moved to Udaipur in the 16th century.

posing temple of Mahadeo within the fort was where Rana Kumbha was murdered by his own son; held in by the ramparts are innumerable palaces, royal apartments and garden pavilions topped by the ethereal Badal Mahal — the lighted beacons of which, on a clear night, could be seen twinkling even from distant Jodhpur.

Akbar's devastation of Chittor and the reigning Maharana Udai Singh's move to the next Sisodia capital led to the creation of Udaipur, the lakeside city built on a small wooded plain encircled by mountains. Carefully built dams around the existing Lake Pichola not only enhanced the beauty of the place but, more importantly, made it easily defensible, for only three passes remained to the valleys below. The Mughal emperor Jehangir failed to breach the defences.

Udaipur's luxurious insouciance provides a direct counterpoise to the aggressive masculinity of Chittor and Kumbhalgarh. Those were cities of war, this a city of peace. Accord with the Mughals was a critical precondition for the transition from the savagery of war to the sensuous celebration of life and beauty that is the very quintessence of Udaipur. The 17th century City Palace sited on a hill beside Lake Pichola rambles across four acres. Visually the impression is of a giant confection; the icing is the riot of arches, domes, turrets, crenellations and kiosks that crown the steep fortress. The imposing exterior walls soaring into the sky evoke memories of Chittor. Within, though, luxurious royal pavilions, the lavish use of marble, a profusion of coloured glass, mirror work, fluted columns, inlay work, silver doors and the formal gardens and fountains reflect a distinct Mughal influence. There was an increased friendliness and interaction with the Mughals after the early 17th century when Maharana Karan Singh struck up friendship and provided sanctuary to the rebellious Khurram, son of Emperor Jehangir, later to become Emperor Shah Jahan. The city palace museum still displays the turbans exchanged between the Mughal and the Sisodia princes in a gesture of friendship. The apartments within the complex are a visual delight, specially Mor Chowk with its intricately crafted, fluorescent blue-green peacock motifs in fine mosaic relief. Badal Mahal is the verdant hilltop garden palace complex built on a ninety feet high natural rock formation; within the palace the visual effect is of elevated rooms that are actually at ground level. Krishna Vilas is the delicate apartment erected to honour the memory of a 19th century teenage Udaipur princess, Krishna Kumari, for whose hand in marriage the houses of Amber and Marwar threatened to go to war.

The resolute princess chose to commit suicide by drinking poison to avert the impending invasions. Her disconsolate father built this apartment decorated with some ravishing miniatures to consecrate her supreme sacrifice. The young princess's act of valour elicited a rather callous witticism from an East India Company official from Calcutta — "Women should die young and by violent means, if they desire the reputation of their beauty to live with posterity. Her story deserves well to be commemorated in a melodrama". An enormous chandelier in the 19th century Kush Mahal vies with the abundance of multi-coloured mirrors to reflect the light. The Chini Chitrashala houses a quaint collection of Chinese porcelain. Flanking Laxmi Vilas Chowk is an art gallery that houses the finest examples of the distinctive Mewar school of painting, with its marvellous depictions of court life that flourished here from the early 18th to the late 19th century.

The pièce de resistance of Udaipur is the 17th century Jag Niwas, a white marble summer palace built in the middle of Lake Pichola by Maharana Jagat Singh. And to think that it was a momentary pique of a petulant prince that was responsible for the construction of a monument so unforgettably picturesque! The story goes that prince Jagat Singh once sought his father Amar Singh's permission to take a party of friends for a of bit of frolic and amusement to the idyllic Jag Mandir pavilions. The father curtly refused permission and further added insult to injury by telling his son to go build his own lake resort if he was so taken up with the place. The Lake Palace of Jag Niwas was the irate Jagat Singh's stinging retort to his crusty father! Set on an island, the whole palace appears to float in the lake like an oriental vision of Xanadu. Within lie profusely-decorated, sumptuously-painted royal suites bathed in a mosaic of light that filters in through coloured glass windows. Pavilions built around limpid pools reflect the blue of a shimmering sky across which flash birds of brilliant plumage. All around is the reflective brightness of sun, sky and lake, stunning views of the statuesque city palace and the verdant green mountains that encircle the lake. Today this palace is one of the most romantic hotel resorts in the world.

Jag Mandir, the other lake palace built for Emperor Shah Jahan when he sought sanctuary at Udaipur has a haunting beauty, its walls made of stone slabs of almost translucent thinness that were once inlaid with jasper, jade and rubies. It has spacious courtyards, domed, high-ceilinged rooms, pleasant formal gardens and arched pavilions em-

Maharana Arvind Singh Mewar of Udaipur with his wife, daughter and son attending the Holi ceremony in which a fire is lit to commemorate the burning of Holika.

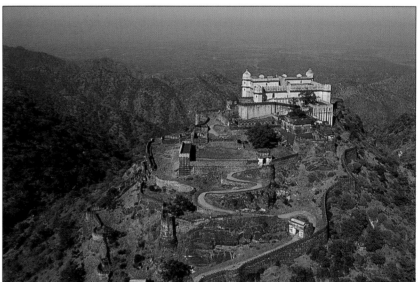

The 15th century Kumbhalgarh fort built by Rana Kumbha, a poignant symbol of Rajput valour.

bellished with fading frescoes open to the breezes of the lake.

The hilltop Sajjangarh palace commands a magnificent view of the city. Beyond the fortification of the city are the charming picnic pavilions of Saheliyon ki Baari, scene of many royal feasts, apparently built for a Sisodia princess who loved the rains. All around the city are lakes — Fatehsagar, and the 19th century Jaisamand (the largest arti-

CELEBRATIONS

Because the landscape was so
monochromatic and harsh, they
set it aflame with the colours of
their raiment — ruby reds, shocking pinks
and crimsons, electric blues and greens. Because beauty seemed so remote in their
parched land, they created it — in their clothes,
jewellery, homes; embellishing and adorn-
ing everything: their camels, themselves, their
kitchen walls, their king's palace. Because
life seemed so short and uncertain, they celebrated it through joyous, exuberant songs
and dances; through festivals of winter, spring
and the blessed rain that brought relief from
the relentless sun.

Then, as now, noble women only wore
gold; others wore silver, and those who could
not afford either wore tattoos. Royal
toshakhanas (treasuries) at Jaipur, Jodhpur,
Jaisalmer, Bikaner, Kotah, and Bundi ex-
tended patronage to innumerable enamellers
and jewellers who pandered to the demands
of the royal *zenana*. Raja Man Singh actually

imported five families of enamellers from distant Lahore to his kingdom of Amber in the 16th century. Today, their descendants in Jaipur continue to fashion intricately-wrought gold jewellery with enamel ornamentation in the champlevé (raised field) technique—a de rigueur item in any self-respecting Rajput bride's trousseau. In obscure bylanes of the old city, young artisans cut and polish rubies, diamonds and emeralds to glittering perfection to be exported to all corners of the world; semi-precious stones can be purchased here for a fraction of the price one would pay in London or New York showrooms.

A sub-art of enamelling in Jaipur is its extension to new mediums like silver and copper. Tiny, bejewelled, enamelled silver elephants make excellent souvenirs; finely-enamelled copper sheets are fashioned into table tops, wall plaques and ornamental bowls.

In the streets Rajasthani women jostle past in swirling, block-printed nine-yard skirts, the brilliant reds and yellows of their mantles setting off their chunky silver jewellery to perfection. The poorest among them will wear a heavy *rakhri* on her forehead, innumerable bone and ivory bangles and heavy anklets, apart from nose, ear and toe-

rings. Their men, dressed in earth colours or white, provide an effective counterpoint, but they too flaunt fine silver and gold necklaces, rings and earrings, giving them the appearance of birds of exotic plumage. Their tattoo motifs provide vital clues to the desert people's psyche; a *kalpavriksha* or tree of life motif on the forearm and a dot denoting Lakshmi, the goddess of wealth, indicate the fierce will to live and prosper.

International fashion designers flock to Jaipur in quest of indigenously designed and printed fabrics that have been exported to the West and the Far East since medieval times. The craftsman's ingenuity and skill never cease to surprise. Before the advent of chemical dyes, they were using (as some still do) vegetable dyes extracted from flowers, bark, roots and minerals. Jasmine, saffron and myrobalan produced oranges and yellows; mulberry bark and the *kirmiz* insect yielded reds and purples, while a deep black was coaxed from iron. Designs reveal a sometimes precise and geometric and at other times a florid, imaginative sensibility. This is reflected in the fabrics available—flowing, diagonal-striped *lahariyas* or the immense variety of tie-and-dye designs from Jaipur, Jodhpur, Bikaner and Udaipur; delicate, hand-block-printed floral sprigs from Sanganer and bold brick-and-black, linear zigzag motifs from Bagru, both near Jaipur; the red-and-indigo *ajrak* from remote Barmer. The motifs are subtle and delicate, the colours almost always stunning—unusual combinations of scarlet and shocking magenta, purple and orange, turquoise and parrot green, often shot with gold and silver and set off with shining mirrors, to be worn by men and women alike as turbans, skirts, veils or saris.

Jaipur has other crafts to offer—chiselled figurines carved from jade, onyx, coral and smoky topaz, as well as statues of marble extracted from the nearby Makrana mines that was once also supplied for the building of the fabled Taj Mahal. Today, stonemasons sculpt the same marble into figures of Hindu gods or planters and ashtrays with the industriousness and vestigial skills—but not the genius—of their Barmer forefathers. It is in Barmer that crafts persons still carve hard, unyielding sandstone with such delicacy that it resembles Venetian lace. Elsewhere in the old city are pit looms where wool and silk carpets of finely-detailed Persian designs are woven for an ever-burgeoning export market. The most fabulous carpets, though, continue to be woven in Bikaner, where the turn-of-the-century ruler Ganga Singh started the industry as a vocation for prisoners. On one occasion a ruling Bikaner potentate actually bought a Persian carpet in London that, on closer examination, turned out to be woven in his own kingdom! An art unique to Bikaner is that of buffing and moulding camel hide to fashion photoframes, perfumed vials, vases and containers, all embellished with gilded gesso-work floral motifs.

Particular to Jaipur is the art of blue pottery, a craft of Persian-Turkish origin. It is distinctive in that clay is substituted with a mixture of fuller's earth, quarrtz and sodium sulphate. The characteristic turquoise blue is derived from copper sulphate, the deep blue comes from cobalt oxide. It is made in moulds, only the neck and lip are turned on the wheel. The finest example of this art can be seen at Rambagh's Polo Bar where an entire fountain has been created in this genre.

In Jaipur, Jodhpur, Bikaner—indeed, all over Rajasthan—you could buy 'classical' miniatures or folk *phad* and *pichhwai* paintings, pale imitations of the splendid originals. *Phads* — finely hand-painted scrolls that were gradually unfurled to the accompaniment of the balladeer's song extolling the virtues of folk heroes—have been substituted by garish, blotchily executed replicas that are at best uninspiring. The miniatures are often coarse and ham-handed, the votive *pichhwais* outright travesties. *Pichhwais* were depictions of Lord Krishna in his various manifestations, usually painted on cloth, to be hung as a backdrop to the deity's image in Nathdwara. Today, Japanese scroll motifs and naive Ajanta frescoes on cloth are palmed off as *pichhwais*; lamentable, but hardly surprising, considering that Jodhpur and Shekhawati have a thriving cottage industry of made-to-order antiques, much sought after by customers who cannot afford the prices of the originals.

But the febrile pulse of Rajasthan throbs fiercest in its vibrant folk songs and dances.

Wizened old bhopas and dholis, traditional singers, chant ditties about folk heroes of yore—Baba Ramdev, Dhola Maru and Gogaji—in voices surprisingly strong and passionate. Performances open with the stirring call of the imposing trumpet, the *bankia*. Musicians use ancient, unsophisticated instruments that produce strangely mesmeric sounds: twin flutes called *algoza*, the hypnotic Jewish harp or *morchang*, the stringed instrument with a tinkling cluster of bells attached called the *ravanhatha* and the earthen pitcher or *matka*, turned in the hands with amazing dexterity and used as a percussion instrument.

The *Kachhi-ghodi* is a particularly vigorous dance in which a bride-groom's party boisterously sings folk ballads and stages a mock-fight with much nimble sidestepping, sharp pirouetting and brandishing of swords; dancers are ensconced within the figure of a horse with just their torsos showing. A statelier dance is the *Ghair*: regal men in fulsome, gathered white ankle-length skirts and brilliant turbans swirl slowly in alternately clockwise and anti-clockwise motions, clicking long, painted sticks with each other, the periodic clash of sticks creating its own fevered cadence. There is

ONE KINGDOM, TWO FIEFDOMS

Bundi, Kota

Rudyard Kipling wrote a poem about a Bundi legend, which is concerned with the mistress of an ancient Bundi ruler. This woman was a dancer, and somewhat looked down on by the palace officials and courtiers. The king died, as all kings must; his wives were supposed to burn themselves on his pyre, but this they showed an understandable disinclination to do. The dancer volunteered to burn with her lord, and did.

— Dom Moraes

The Chattar Mahal Palace at Bundi seen from Taragarh fort above. The palace seems to grow out of the hillside and possibly even into it.

Top: The Elephant Gate at City Palace, Kota. Elephants are a leitmotif in Hadoti architecture as is evident in most Bundi and Kota buildings.
Above: The Jag Mandir at Kota.
Facing page: Maharaja Brij Raj Singh and his consort, in their Brijraj Palace, a part of which has now been converted into a hotel.

The quiet mountain kingdom of Bundi was founded in the 14th century by the Hara branch of the Chauhan Rajputs, whom the Muslim invader Mohammad Ghori vanquished and drove out from Delhi in 1192. Rao Dev Hara set out in 1342 to the mountainous terrain of Bundi, where after a fierce engagement with the local Bhil chieftain, he succeeded in establishing a kingdom for his dispossessed people.

The Chittor Rajputs never forgave Rao Dev Hara for his acquisition of a territory that they traditionally regarded as part of their own domain, and Bundi's history for the next three hundred years was one of constant skirmishes with their erstwhile mentors. The newly-powerful neighbourhood kingdom of Amber, flushed with its military and political triumphs and position of pre-eminence at the Mughal court, also eyed Bundi covetously.

Peace and relative stability only came to turbulent Bundi in the 16th century, when Rao Suryan Hara accepted Mughal overlordship in return for guarantees of religious freedom and imperial honours. In a befitting recognition of services rendered, the 17th century Rao Chattrasal, hero of 52 battles, was accorded a rare honour by Shah Jahan—the governorship of Delhi.

The 18th and 19th centuries were peaceful. Amber treacherously attacked and conquered the kingdom all too briefly, but Rao Umaid Singh retrieved Bundi by securing the assistance of the powerful Holkar ruler of Indore, whose palms he had to grease liberally for the purpose. By 1878 Bundi had come under British tutelage and, inevitably, went into political eclipse.

Today Bundi radiates a pearly luminiscence that reflects none of the turbulence of its past. The 14th century Taragarh fort sprawls atop a 500 ft hill, an awesome monument that historian Tod rated as one of the finest in Rajputana. Bhim Burj is the imposing tower that once housed the huge 16th century Garbh Ganjam cannon; adjacent to this is a well into which the soldier would leap to protect his eardrums once the fuse had been lit! Within the fort are pavilions that tell of a colourful, often violent past—the arsenal where gunpowder was manufactured for the Garbh Ganjam; a shrine to Shiva under a carved canopy supported by elephant brackets; a serene Ram Mahal reflected in a large water tank and a deserted pavilion. Legend has it that within the twisted caverns in the hills of Taragarh lies a fabulous treasure. At Taragarh too, folklore would have us believe, are the underground tunnels through which the rulers could escape.

Rao Chattrasal shifted from the hilltop Taragarh fort to the plains below, where he built Chattar Mahal, a palace in the traditional Rajput style with its drooping arcuate roof, carvings of lotuses and sculpted elephants guarding its Hathiya Pol entrance.

MAVERICKS, MARAUDERS, MONARCHS

Bharatpur, Deeg, Alwar

I was sitting next to Mountbatten at a dinner party and he said, 'You have still not acceded.' There was dead silence at the dinner table. After dinner I said, 'You're accusing me, but may I also remind you that the British gave me restricted powers, not allowing me to sign or do anything without the Viceroy's permission; now do I have your permission to sign the Instrument of Accession?' and within twenty-four hours I got my powers!

— Maharaja of Bharatpur
(as told to Charles Allen)

Yuvraj (crown prince) Vishwendra Singh of Bharatpur with his son in the garden of his early-20th century Golbagh Palace residence whose architecture combines features from the Rajput, Mughal and art nouveau traditions.

Top: Interior of one of the summer palaces at Deeg, near Bharatpur.
Above: The 18th-century Gopal Bhavan at Deeg overlooks Gopal Sagar.
Facing page: Yuvrani Divya Singh of Bharatpur in her traditional finery. On her head she wears a diamond-studded gold borla *and around her neck an exquisitely-wrought antique suite of diamonds and rubies.*

Bharatpur was the only Jat kingdom of any consequence in India. The Jats' transition from humble peasantry to royal pageantry and ultimately to dissolution and inevitable oblivion was accomplished in the short space of three hundred years. During this time span they won and lost a huge swathe of territory between Agra and Delhi, switched allegiance from the Mughals to the Marathas to the British and managed to build a fairly invincible fort as well as palaces and hunting lodges that reflected various influences — Rajput, Mughal and art-nouveau.

The story of Bharatpur begins with Churaman, the late 17th century Jat chieftain who united his clansmen against the increasingly weak Mughals who after suffering a few raids on their territories retaliated by inflicting a humiliating defeat on Churaman that culminated with having his devastated stronghold "ploughed over by asses". But his successor Badan Singh refused to buckle down and by 1751 was a powerful ruler controlling a large territory in the Agra-Delhi region and whose primacy was accorded tacit recognition by the ruling Mughal monarch. He was granted the royal insignia of honour, the *mahi maratib* and the kingdom was made hereditary. An 18th century successor, Surajmal, stormed Agra, pillaged the Taj Mahal from where he carried away silver doors, whole panels of marble inlaid with precious stones and was marching towards Delhi — already reeling under the impact of successive Maratha and Afghan depredations — when he was slain in battle near Agra by avenging Mughal forces.

Bharatpur met its nemesis in 1803 when it made a gross political miscalculation by switching sides to the Marathas in the ongoing British-Maratha war. A furious Lord Lake, determined to teach Bharatpur a lesson, besieged Lohagarh — the iron fort — and "suffered the largest losses experienced by the British in India" till that period in terms of men and expense. More to the point, he won and the British powerhold over Bharatpur tightened. A succession of effete rulers speeded the kingdom's descent into oblivion. Randhir Singh's obsession with lavatorial rather than gubernatorial concerns was legendary — the constipated monarch apparently spent over six hours a day in his toilet from where he heard petitions and delivered summary judgements. An even more whimsical successor bought up fleets of Rolls Royces to collect municipal rubbish and squandered the fast-depleting royal fortunes on hosting huge viceregal parties for the legendary Bharatpur duck shoots.

The period of empire-building and consolidation in the mid-18th century and early 19th century coincided with an explosion of building activity. The 18th century Lohagarh is today swamped by the city rubble but its

FEALTY

She sweeps into the room; the Silk Cut cigarettes, lighter and chilled lemonade follow on a silver salver. "Or would you prefer a cup of tea ?" The accent is expensive private school, the manners impeccable but distant, the hauteur unmistakeable. At seventy plus, the lady radiates mystique. Only traces remain of the legendary beauty but the woman has a rivetting presence that can still reduce one to a mumbling heap! You are in the presence of Rajmata Gayatri Devi of Jaipur, once rated by *Vogue* as one of the ten most beautiful women of the world.

Yesterday's pursuits were more luxurious — which blue diamond to wear tonight, St. Moritz or Monaco for the summer... Today's pursuits are more varied, eclectic, meaningful. She is in the forefront of the 'Keep Jaipur Beautiful' movement ("My dear, they wanted to demolish the old city walls and the gateways. I wrote to Nehru who

Preceding page:
Maharaja Swaroop Singh,
paternal uncle of
Maharaja Gaj Singh, with
his wife, Maharani Usha
Kumari, and son in the
drawing room of his Ajit
Bhavan Palace.
Preceding page, inset:
Anirudh Singh Sinsinvar,
heir-apparent, Bharatpur,
in festive finery.
Above: Thakur Narain
Singh of Kanota ties a
turban on his young son's
head.

promptly issued orders to stop what he agreed would be a sacrilege".), is very involved with her two schools and the craft centre through which she has helped revive the traditional art of blue pottery. Enquiries about a self-aborted political career that began with a record-breaking Guinness Book victory over the ruling Congress party, and ended with her imprisonment by Indira Gandhi, meet an enigmatic response. You ask if Indira felt 'insecure', had any 'threat perception' from her. The answer comes with the characteristic prefix : "My dear, *that* question is really not for me to answer".

The woman who broke *purdah*, started the first girl's school in Rajasthan, and broke almost every rule in the 'Conservative Rajput Woman's Guide to Living' book, is dismissive, even angry, about any allusions to her being the epitome of radical chic in the early 1940s of royal Rajasthan. "Stuff and nonsense", she expostulates. "I was always in *purdah*. What rules did I break ? Long before my arrival, Her Highness Jodhpur was riding out in slacks for shoots, vacationing in En-

gland, shopping at Harrods". What of her cosmopolitanism ? The extensive travelling in Europe as a teenager, the chic hi-society to-do's she patented the art of throwing in her opulent Rambagh Palace residence ? The answer comes in a firm tone that discourages further probing. "That", she answers frostily, "was all too common among royal families. Girls of our background had English governesses and travelled abroad often enough. What parties ? I was too busy with my charities and the Red Cross — there was a World War on in case you didn't know!" The past is hopefully buried and forgotten; today she has her eyes trained on posterity. The radical would like to be known as the conformist. But then, Gayatri Devi is the very personification of contradiction. The most abiding image of royalty, she is ironically enough two-thirds common if you follow her genealogical chart. A maternal grandfather from Baroda came from peasant stock, her paternal grandmother was Brahmo while her husband was adopted from the noble family of Isarda near Jaipur. But such is the royal air

she exudes that you just cannot call her Mrs Gayatri Devi. You could legislate the title into oblivion but not the charisma.

Today's royal battles are fought with income tax authorities from whose constant depredations, dwindling inheritances are constantly guarded. Eton and Oxford educated maharajas a la Gaj Singh Jodhpur or the widely travelled Arvind Singh Udaipur and Brijraj Singh Kotah have managed to integrate royal savoir faire with great marketing savvy to turn huge liabilities into profitable assets. Gaj Singh of the magnificent kohl-rimmed 'Jodhpur' eyes as maharaja-in-residence at the pink Umaid Bhawan Palace is as huge a draw as the turn of the century art deco suites that are the unique selling proposition of his desert palace. Arvind Singh Udaipur's ancestors may have gone over body counts at Haldighati; his own interest veers more towards tabulating profit figures on the Lake Palace hotel's balance sheets. Brijraj Singh Kotah and his beautiful wife — a Coochbehar princess — affect the works (turbans, pearls, diamonds and chiffons) for the mandatory 'hard sell' royal picture. The Maharani of Kotah, coiffured stiff, stands stoically besides her dashing consort and suffers the glare of arc-lights and camera flashes. It is not the Brijraj Palace but the ambience that sells — an ambience they are only too aware they alone can provide. These are modern monarchs, at once directors and protagonists in an ongoing drama of the Raj and tax trouble- ridden opulence.

Clearly the times-are-a-changing. Gayatri Devi remembers being 'appalled' at her late husband's decision to convert Rambagh Palace into a hotel; today she salutes his foresight. Fellow His Highnesses known to make rather acid comments on 'those Jaipur carpet-baggers' ate humble pie and followed suit soon enough once the message went home — royalty sells! Whether at Kotah, Jodhpur, Bikaner, Jaisalmer or Udaipur, out came the family silver, vintage Persian carpets were unfurled, solid teak furniture was polished to high-gloss perfection and gilt-edged sepia portraits of great aunts and uncles, glamorous nephews and nieces were

The noble house of Shahpura, close to Jaipur. Such fiefs once owed allegiance to former princely states and contributed to their revenues as well as their army.

Top: The heir-apparent of Udaipur—Lakshyaraj Singh—with attendants, all wearing the distinctive flat-topped Udaipur turbans. Occasionally the little prince likes to play the drums with the Palace band at Shiv Niwas.
Right: Thakur Sajjan Singh of Ghanerao, a fief that owed allegiance to both Udaipur and Jodhpur.

displayed upon mantlepieces in freshly re-painted rooms as artefacts to provide the all-important atmosphere in residences that are now as much deluxe hotels as museums.

The aristocracy was quick to imitate royalty. Thakur Sajjan Singh runs Ghanerao Palace Hotel en route from Jodhpur to Udaipur; Thakur Devi Singh runs the Mandawa Palace Hotel in Shekhawati while Maharaja Swaroop Singh, uncle to Maharaja Gaj Singh Jodhpur, runs Ajit Bhawan, his residence, as a hugely successful hotel.

Commercial pursuits have sometimes, if not always, been accompanied by a certain crassness of the spirit.

Yesterday's monarch is today's mealy-mouthed merchant. But there are saving graces, nevertheless. Gaj Singh Jodhpur turned down a lucrative profit sharing deal with an international hotel chain when they made the termination of the services of a hundred old retainers a pre-requisite for signing the contract. His explanation — "How could I abandon my people? They have served the family for generations."

Historical contexts might have changed, the ethos certainly has not. You glean that through the occasional vignette, the sudden display of a whimsicality. These are revelations that are sometimes poignant, at other times arch, but many a time plain hilarious.

The 15th century fort of Neemrana was sold to a Bania businessmen conglomerate; the destitute royal moved down to the base of the very hill where the family's proud flag once fluttered. What stood forsaken was not mere possessions but even memories of his glorious past — the black and white pictures of family weddings and celebrations that now constitute the hotel's decor were also part of the sale. The present has no future — the past with its memories bartered for a handful of silver.

A long-time observer of Rajputana royalty offers an illuminating insight — "It would seem the Rajput's history today is not one of past glories but of past grievances". The house of Udaipur never sent a princess as ransom to the Mughal bed. To date Udaipur royalty is not averse to rubbing that fact in while making acid comments on Jaipur and other royal houses that did so. "Can't really call them Rajputs", drawls one, "not after the way they traded their women with those Turks". Gayatri Devi's response to that is tart, equally cutting. "My dear, that argument really is tiresome. I mean, how archaic can you get. Let's not even discuss that".

The memory of that first ignoble Rajput-Mughal matrimonial trade-off obviously rankles — probably as much now as it did then. The average Jaipur

Left: Thakur Yaduvendra Singh of Samode in the frescoed interiors of his Samode Haveli in Jaipur.

103

noble will still offer facile explanations to dismiss the fact as a mere 'historical misconception' — "Of course it wasn't a Jaipur princess that was married to Akbar, it was only a common girl born out of concubinage". It is a twisted sort of pride that you may or may not understand!

Elsewhere the bloody fraticidal wars rage on even today as at Udaipur where the royal brothers Mahendra Singh and Arvind Singh squabble bitterly over a title—Maharana—that now exists only notionally. But what resounding titles! The Kishangarh ruler's long-winding one is a case in instance: Umdae Rajahe Bulund Mukam Laiqul Inayat Sadiq ul Durham Maharajadhiraj Maharaja Brijraj Singh! Reinforced with the thirteen, nineteen, twenty-one gun salutes, these to many royals were worth dying for — a fact the British shrewdly capitalised on.

But there are always the lighter moments. An impetuous descendant of the proud Shekhawat clan whose ancestors once put the fear of god into Jaipur, gets drunk, then enraged over a fancied insult, wrenches a sword off the wall where it is displayed and proceeds to slash his wrists in a spectacular display of Rajput-harakiri rage. He is rushed to hospital for the mandatory stitches where he does a Houdini act and is discovered after much sleuthing cowering in a dark corridor. "No stitches for me", shouts our moustachioed Rajput warrior in a quaking voice, "they hurt too much!" Sword-smart, needle-nettled?

These are mere images and not necessarily those that provide a complete picture of the living feudals. Today they are a race trying to come to grips not so much with the past as with the present. The future seems uncertain but the feisty spirit that carried them through bloody wars will surely carry them through this present turbulence and help reconcile the constant paradoxes that confront them in their everyday lives. Through it all they have retained a quality of grace, a quiet dignity and a not unjustifiable pride in their tradition. People that once made history now loiter on its very margins but does that negate their earlier contributions? This is the story of royal Rajasthan — of a colourful, passionate people that once ruled huge empires and stories of whose lives and deeds constitute the real romance of this desert country.

Thus grew the tale of wonderland
Thus slowly one by one
Its quaint events were hammered out
And now the tale is done.

Photo Credits

PRAMOD KAPOOR: Jacket cover (front and back). Pages 1, 2-3 (14 pictures), 4-5, 6-7, 9 (top), 10 (bottom), 11 (bottom), 20, 26-27, 28-29 (top and bottom), 30-31, 32 (top and bottom), 33, 34-35, 36-37 , 38, 46-47, 49 (bottom), 53, 54-55, 56, 57, 58 (top and bottom), 59 (top and bottom), 60-61, 62 (top and bottom), 63, 64, 65 (left, top to bottom; middle, top to bottom), 77 (top), 78-79, 81 (top and bottom), 82 (left and right), 84-85, 86 (top and bottom),87, 88-89, 90, 91, 92-93, 94 (top) , 95, 98-99, 99 (inset), 102 (bottom), 103 (bottom).
KAROKI LEWIS: Pages 2-3 (5 pictures), 8 (top and bottom), 9 (bottom), 14,15, 16-17, 18-19, 21, 23, 24, 25 (middle), 39, 40-41, 43, 48 (top and bottom), 49 (top), 65 (right bottom), 80 (except second from top), 83 (middle), 100, 101.
PANKAJ RAKESH: Pages 2-3 (2 pictures), 10-11 (top), 66-67, 68 (top), 69 (top and bottom), 70, 71, 72-73, 74 (top), 75 (top and bottom), 78 (inset), 102-103 (top).
RAJPAL SINGH: Pages 2-3 (3 pictures), 25 (all pictures except the one in the middle), 65 (right middle).
SUBHASH BHARGAVA: Pages 22 (bottom), 26 (inset), 65, (right top), 81 (both middle pictures), 82-83 (middle), 83 (far right), 97.
ADITYA PATANKAR: Pages 12-13, 50-51.
GANESH SAILI: Pages 52, 72 (bottom).
GOPI GAJWANI: Page 22 (top).
N.P.SINGH: Page 80 (second from top).
RAGHUBIR SINGH: Page 94 (bottom).

Lustre Press acknowledges the assistance provided by Mahendra Singh Nagar of the Mehrangarh Museum Trust, Jodhpur, for permission to take and use photographs of Rajasthani turbans.